# CROSSWORDS FOR KIDS MINECRAFT EDITION

Copyright © 2017 Puzzle Time Publishing
All rights reserved

## NOT AN OFFICIAL MINECRAFT PRODUCT. NOT APPROVED BY OR ASSOCIATED WITH MOJANG.

No part of this publication may be reproduced, distributed, or transmitted in any form or by any means, including photocopying, recording, or other electronic or mechanical methods without prior written permission from Puzzle Time Publishing. Pictures may not be duplicated by anyone without express permission.

This book is not authorized or endorsed by or affiliated with Minecraft or Mojang or any of its subsidiaries. All Minecraft references are used in accordance with the Fair Use Doctrine and are not meant to imply that this book is a Minecraft product for advertising or other commercial purposes. All aspects of the game including characters, their names, locations, and other features of the game within this book are trademarked and owned by their respective owners.

# 1 Crossword

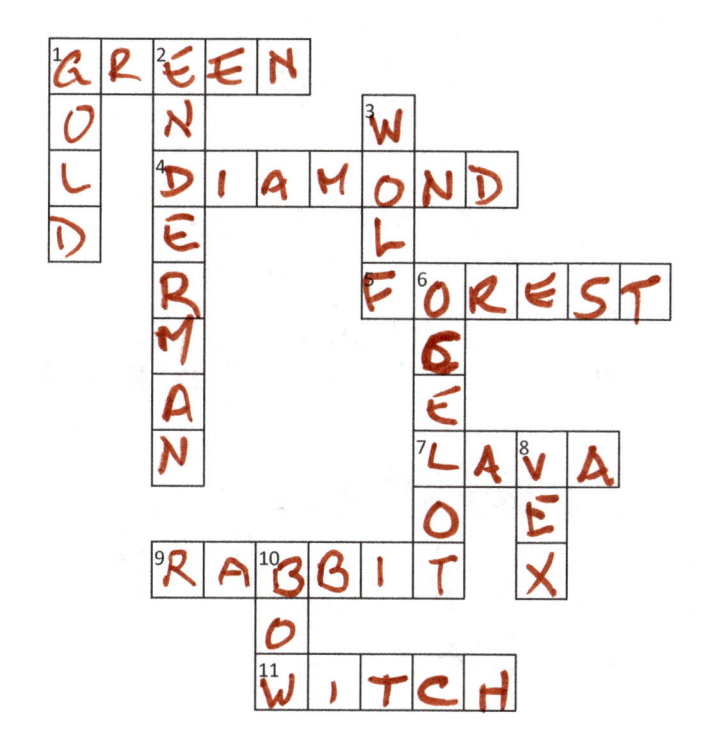

**Across**
1. The color of a creeper (5)
4. What the best swords and armor are made of (7)
5. A biome with lots of trees (6)
7. Hot orange liquid that can kill a player (4)
9. Cute passive mob which hops and has long ears (6)
11. Hostile mob which looks a bit like a villager (5)

**Down**
1. Precious metal you can use to make swords and armor (4)
2. Tall black neutral mob which can teleport (8)
3. Mob you tame with a bone. You can put them in love mode to breed puppies (4)
6. Mob you can tame with raw fish (6)
8. Flying hostile mob which the evoker can summon (3)
10. Weapon which fires arrows (3)

# 2 Quizword

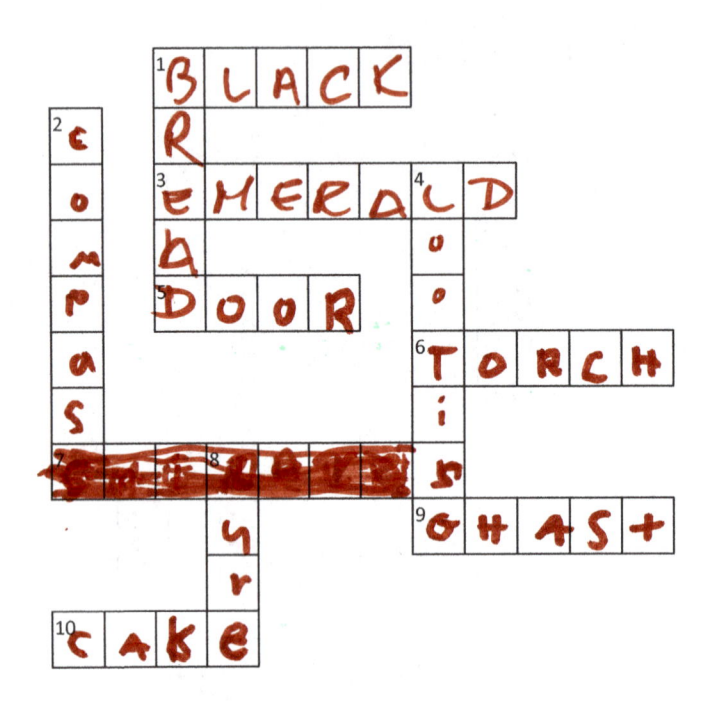

**Across**
1 What color is an Enderman? (5)
3 What gemstone do villagers like to trade with? (7)
5 What does a Minecraft player walk through to get in and out of a building? (4)
6 You use this item to light things up. It's crafted from a stick and coal or charcoal. What is it? (5)
7 What undead mob is really afraid of wolves? (8)
9 What is this Nether mob? Clue: it floats and wails! (5)
10 What yummy food can you craft from milk, sugar, egg and wheat? (4)

**Down**
1 What food item can you craft with 3 wheat? (5)
2 This item points to the world spawn. You craft it using redstone and 4 iron ingots. What is it? (7)
4 What enchantment gives you more drops when you defeat mobs? (7)
8 What enchantment makes more fish bite your hook when you are fishing? (4)

# 3 Crossword

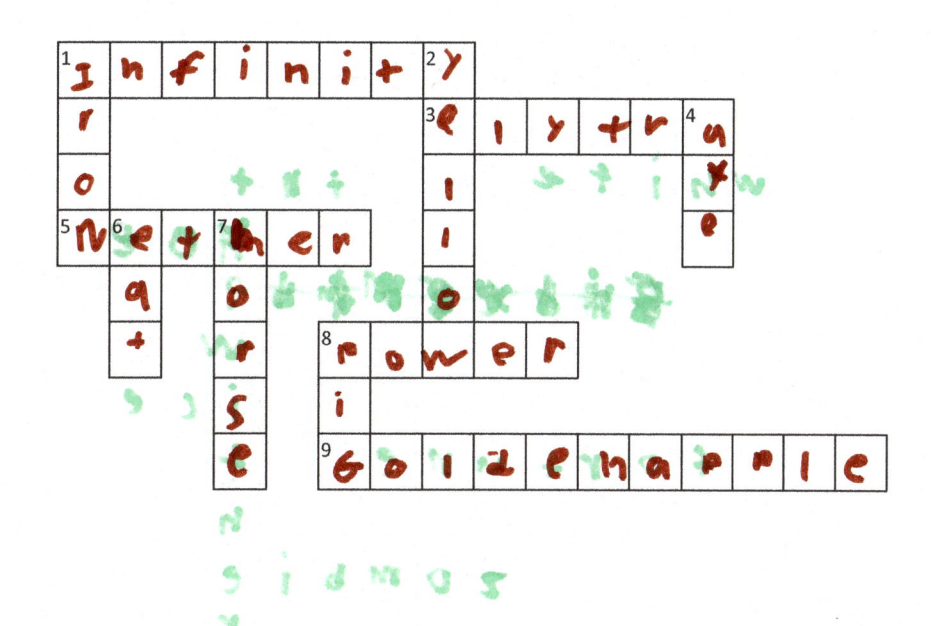

### Across
1. Enchantment which lets you fire arrows as many times as you like without running out (8)
3. An item that's a bit like wings (6)
5. Dimension which has lava, ghasts and blazes (6)
8. Enchantment which increases damage from arrows (5)
9. Special food item crafted using an apple and gold ingots (6,5)

### Down
1. Metal which you can use for crafting weapons. It's a sort of silvery color (4)
2. The color of dandelions and sunflowers (6)
4. Useful tool if you want to collect wood (3)
6. What you need to do to reduce hunger (3)
7. Tameable mob which you can ride and which can also have its own armor (5)
8. Rideable passive mob which drops porkchops when killed (3)

# 4 Crossword

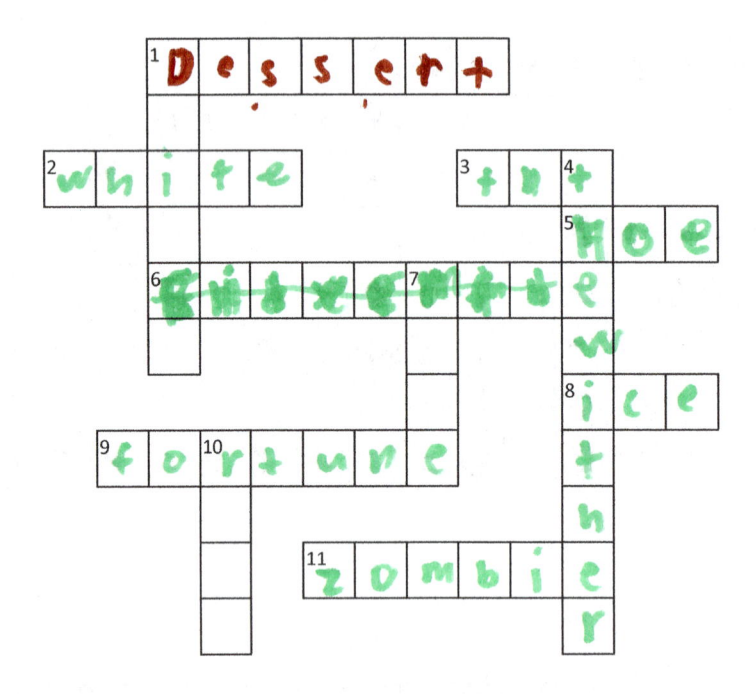

**Across**
1. Flat dry biome with acacia trees (7)
2. The color of snow (5)
3. A block you can use to make an explosion (initials) (3)
5. A tool which you use to till dirt and grass blocks into farmland blocks (3)
6. Very small hostile mob (9) endermite
8. Frozen water (3)
9. Enchantment which increases block drops (7)
11. Undead mob that villagers are really scared of (6)

**Down**
1. Neutral mob with 8 legs (6)
2. Boss mob with three heads (3,6)
7. A tameable mob which can carry chests (4)
10. A non-solid block which you can put a minecart on to allow it to travel (4)

# 5 Crossword

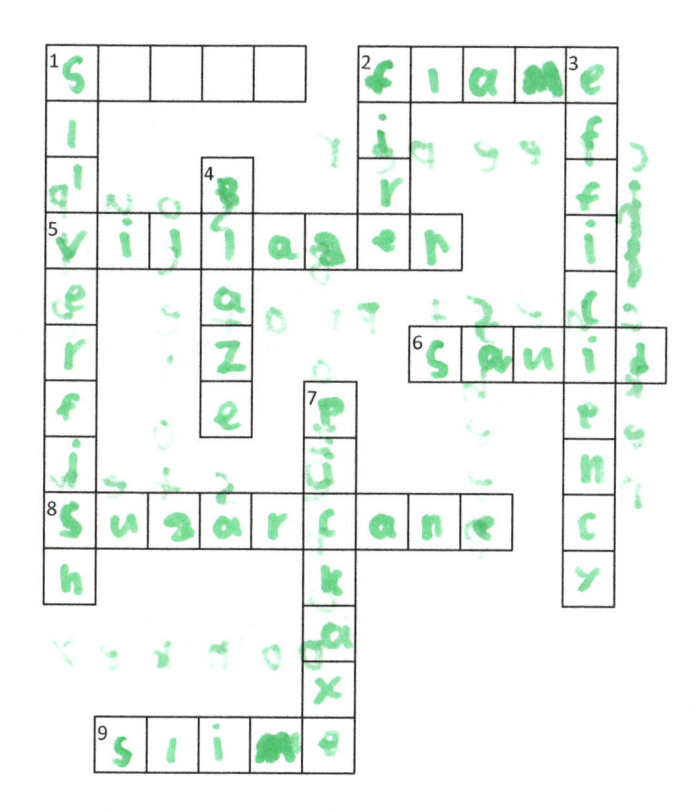

### Across
1 Skeleton which shoots tipped arrows (5)
2 Enchantment which makes arrows turn into flaming arrows (5)
5 NPC who lives in a village and will often trade with players (8)
6 Passive mob which lives in water (5)
8 Item, which grows naturally, that you can use to craft paper (5,4)
9 Green hostile mob shaped like a cube (5)

### Down
1 Little grayish bug-like hostile mob (10)
2 Something that a player can start using a flint and steel (4)
3 Enchantment for tools like pickaxes and shovels, which increases mining speed (10)
4 Fiery hostile Nether mob (5)
7 Really useful tool for mining (7)

# 6 Quizword

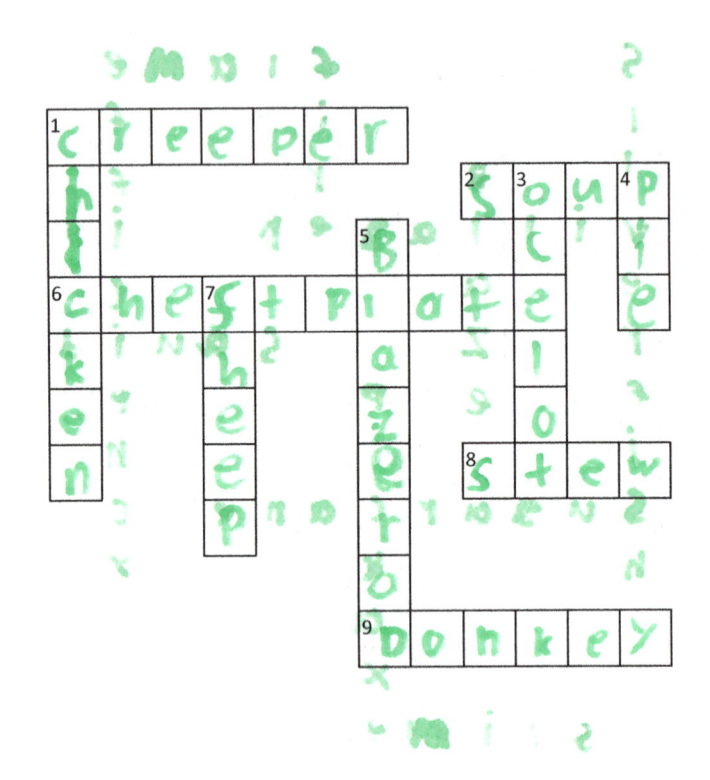

### Across
1 What green mob sneaks up on players and explodes? (7)
2 What food item can you drink? You can make it from beetroot (4)
6 What item of armor does a player wear on their chest? (10)
8 What food item comes in a rabbit or mushroom version? (4)
9 What tameable mob can be used to carry chests? (6)

### Down
1 What passive mob drops a food item, plus sometimes items you need if you want to craft arrows? (7)

3 What passive mob comes in three varieties when it's tamed: tabby, tuxedo

4 Fill in the blanks: a food item that you craft from pumpkin, sugar and egg is a pumpkin pie (3)

5 What stick-shaped item can be dropped by a blaze? (5,3)

7 What passive mob can be sheared to get wool? (5)

# 7 Crossword

|   | 1 R | 2 a | b | b | i | t |   |   |   |   |   |
|---|---|---|---|---|---|---|---|---|---|---|---|
|   |   | r |   |   |   |   | 3 C |   | 4 B | e | e | c | h |
|   | 6 C | r | a | f | t |   | o |   | a |   | o |
|   |   | o |   |   |   | 7 P | o | t | a | t | o | w |
|   | 8 S | w | o | r | 9 d |   | k |   |   |   |   |
|   |   | s |   |   | y |   |   |   |   |   |   |
|   |   |   |   | 10 E | v | 11 o | k | e | r |   |   |
|   |   |   |   |   |   | a |   |   |   |   |   |
|   |   |   |   |   |   | k |   |   |   |   |   |

**Across**

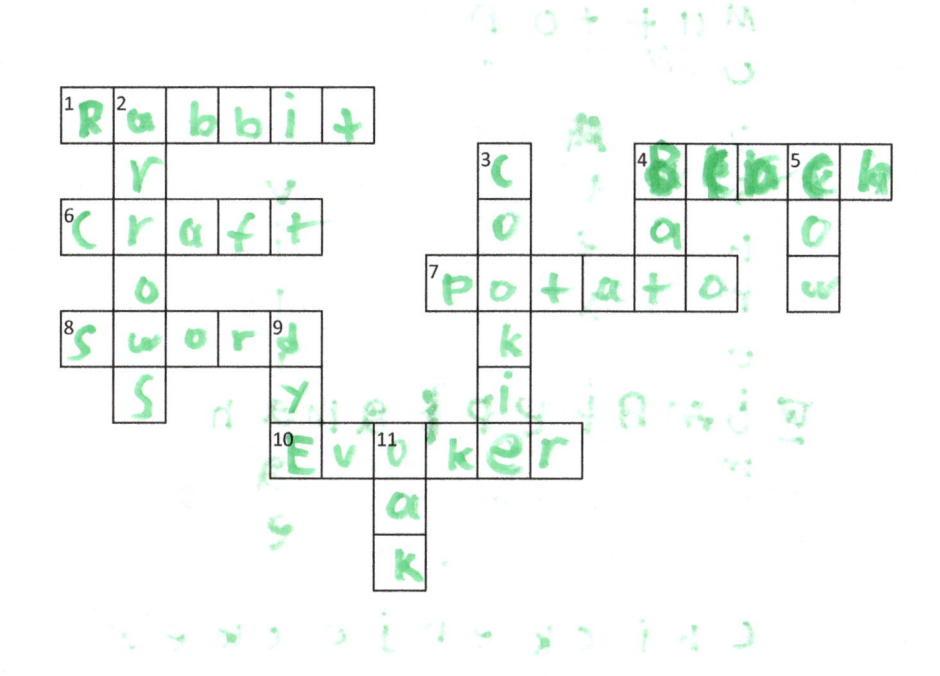

1 This passive mob also comes in a "killer" version (6)
4 A species of tree (5)
6 What you do when you combine things to make something new (5)
7 A food item. You can eat it raw or cooked but make sure it's not poisonous! (6)
8 A weapon you can use in melee combat (5)
10 This hostile mob has the ability to summon vexes (6)

**Down**

2 The ammunition which you fire out of a bow (6)
3 Yummy food which you craft from wheat and cocoa beans (6)
4 Passive mob that flies (3)
5 Farm animal which drops raw beef when it dies (3)
9 Stuff you use to change something's color (3)
11 A species of tree (3)

# 8 Crossword

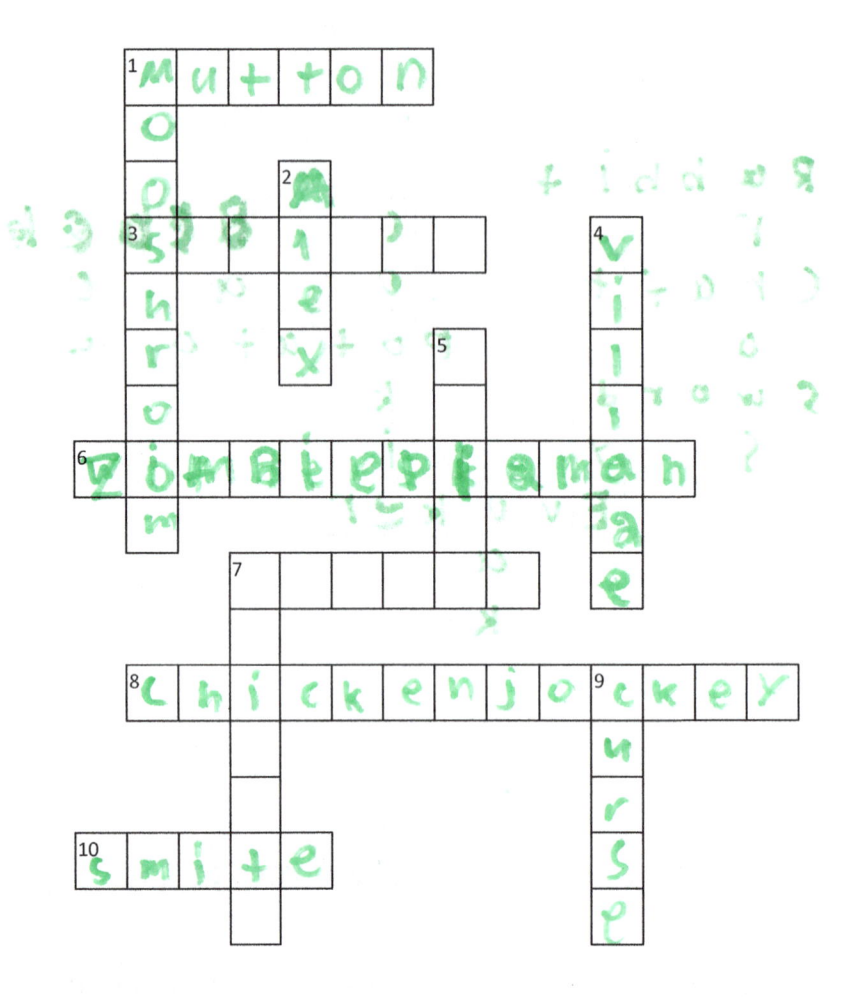

**Across**
1 Food item you can get from a passive mob which drops wool (6)
3 Hostile mob with a purple shell (7)
6 Undead neutral Nether mob (6,6)
7 Kind of mob that includes zombies and skeletons (6)
8 Baby zombie riding on a chicken (7,6)
10 Enchantment that increases damage to undead mobs (5)

**Down**
1 Cow-like passive mob which spawns in mushroom island biomes (9)
2 Steve's friend! (4)
4 Place where villagers live (7)
5 Mostly flat biome with a forest of spruce trees (5)
7 Kind of mob that includes golems (7)
9 Fill in the blank: The enchantment that causes an item to be destroyed when the player dies is the curse of vanishing (5)

# 9 Quizword

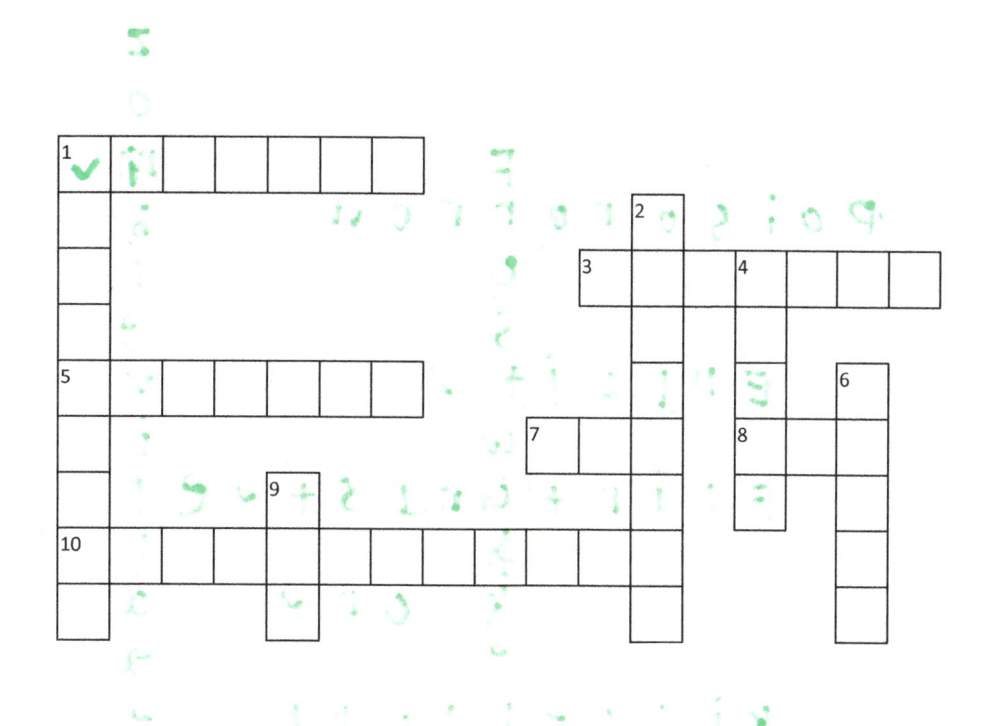

**Across**

1 The Vindicator, Evoker and Illusioner are all types of what? (7)

3 What item is needed for a golem's head? (7)

5 Fill in the blanks: an enchantment which stops a cursed item being removed is the curse of _ _ _ _ _ _ _ (7)

7 What color are a spider's eyes? (3)

8 What do you call an ocelot when it has been tamed? (3)

10 What enchantment increases your luck when you fish? (4,2,3,3)

**Down**

1 What achievement do you get when you eat rotten flesh? (4,5)

2 What underwater hostile mob spawns in and around ocean monuments? (8)

4 What enchantment gives a higher level of knockback? (5)

6 What is the name of the main Minecraft character? (5)

9 Fill in the blanks: When you need to catch fish, you use a fishing _ _ _ (3)

# 10 Crossword

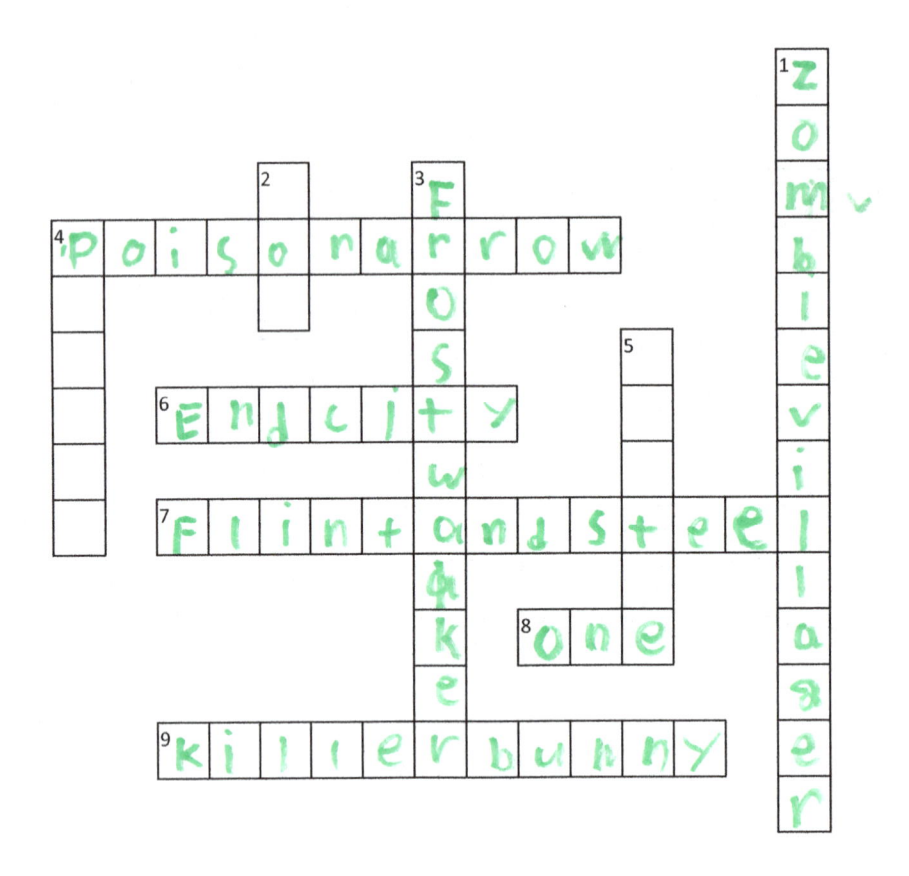

**Across**

4 Poisoned kind of arrow (6,5)

6 City located in The End (3,4)

7 Item for lighting fires (5,3,5)

8 The number of cakes you can craft using one egg, three milk, three wheat and two sugar (3)

9 Dangerous rabbit (6,5)

**Down**

1 Undead mob that looks like a villager (6,8)

2 The color which a blue sheep turns when it's affected by an evoker's sheep conversion spell (3)

3 Enchantment that turns water to ice when you walk on it (5,6)

4 The place where the Ender Dragon can spawn (3,3)

5 Fill in the blanks: If you want to store a potion you can put it in a glass bottle (6)

# 11 Quizword

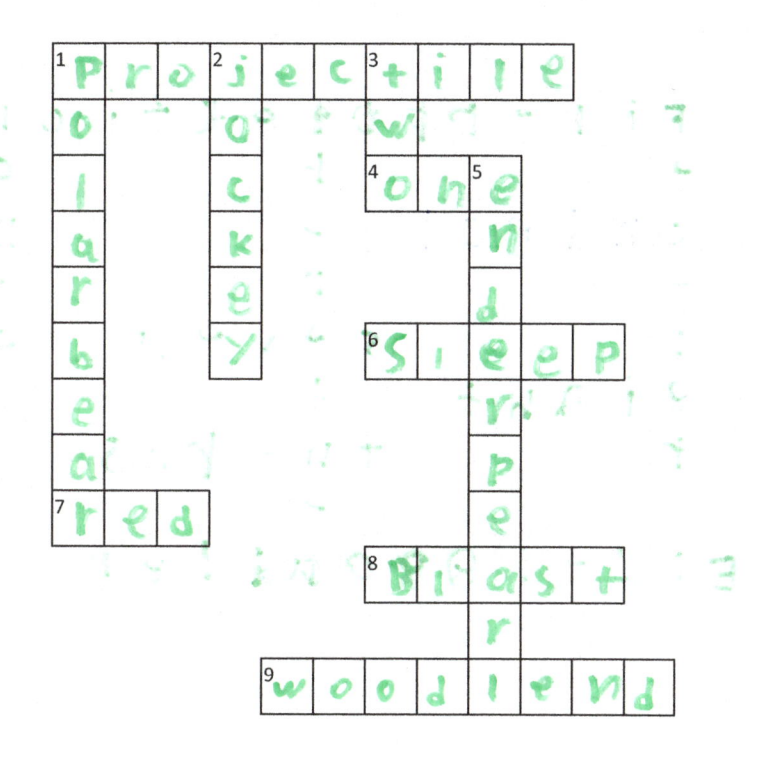

### Across

1 Fill in the blanks: an enchantment that reduces damage from things like arrows is called __projectile__ protection (10)

4 How many sticks are there in the crafting recipe for a sword? (3)

6 What can a player do overnight in a bed? (5)

7 What color is a poppy? (3)

8 Fill in the blanks: an armor enchantment which reduces damage from explosions is called __blast__ protection (5)

9 What is the name of the kind of mansion where evokers and vindicators naturally spawn? (8)

### Down

1 What neutral mob is found in really cold places? (5,4)

2 What is the name for a mob riding on a spider or a chicken? (6)

3 How many cakes can you craft using 2 eggs, 6 milk, 6 wheat and 4 sugar? (3)

5 What teleporting item can sometimes be found in a stronghold altar chest? (5,5)

# 12 Crossword

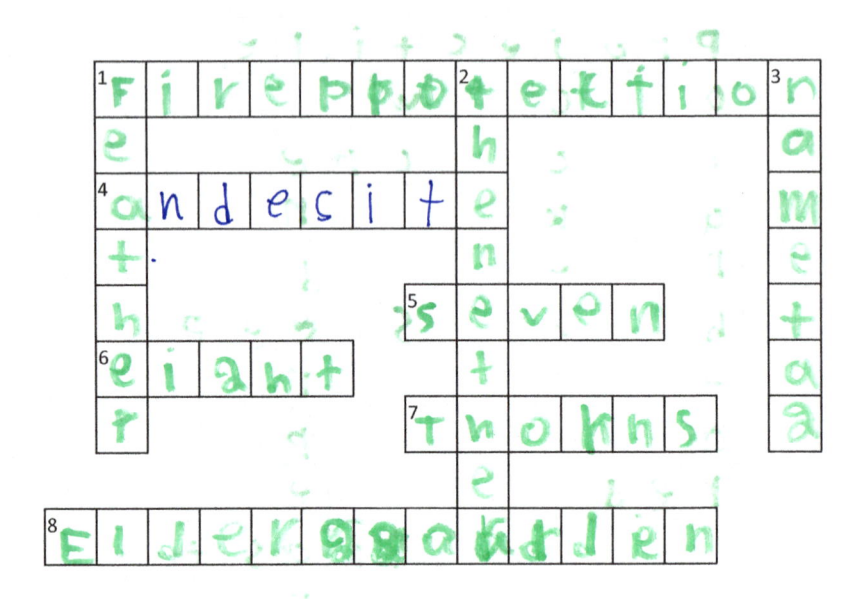

**Across**
1 This enchantment reduces damage taken from fire (4,10)
4 This block is a type of rock which is grey in color (8)
5 The number of gold ingots needed to craft gold leggings (5)
6 The number of iron ingots you need to craft an iron chestplate (5)
7 This armor enchantment causes damage to anything attacking the player (6)
8 Hostile mob found in ocean monuments which has an ability to inflict mining fatigue (5,8)

**Down**
1 Arrow crafting ingredient obtained from a chicken (7)
2 The place where you can find magma cubes, zombie pigmen and wither skeletons (3,6)
3 Item you can use to name a mob (4,3)

# 13 Crossword

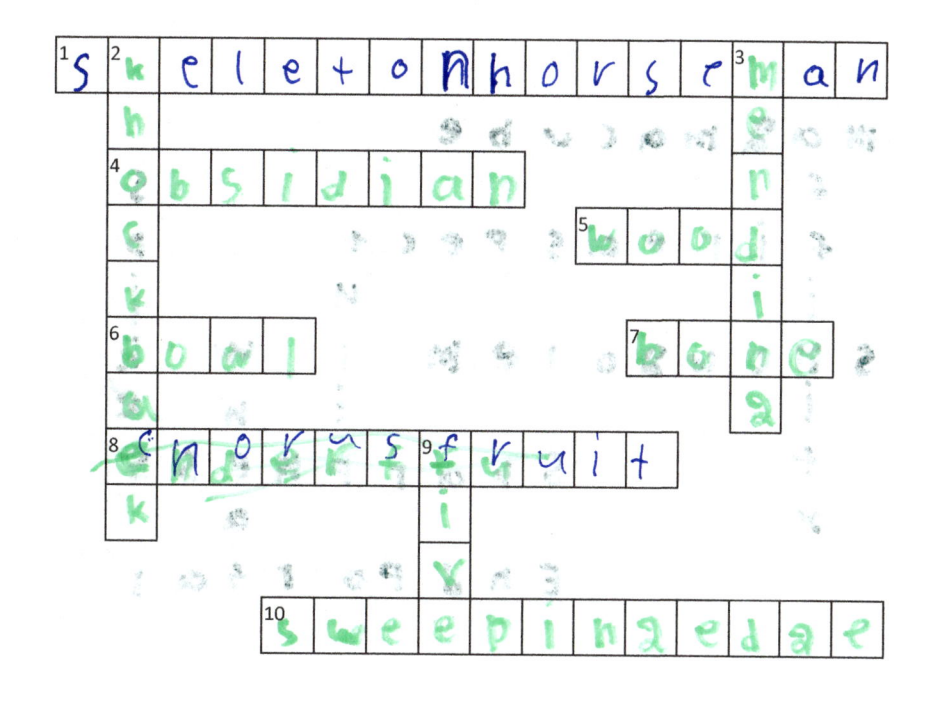

## Across
1 Undead rider and horse (8,8)
4 Block which can be created using lava and water (8)
5 Naturally occurring substance which you can get from trees (4)
6 Useful item if you want to put mushroom stew or beetroot soup in it (4)
7 Item you can use to tame a wolf (4)
8 Type of fruit which can cause teleportation (6,5)
10 Enchantment which increases the damage inflicted for each hit from a sweep attack (8,4)

## Down
2 Enchantment which causes an increase in knockback (9)
3 Enchantment which uses experience to repair an item's durability (7)
9 The number of iron ingots you would need to craft an iron helmet (9)

# 14 Quizword

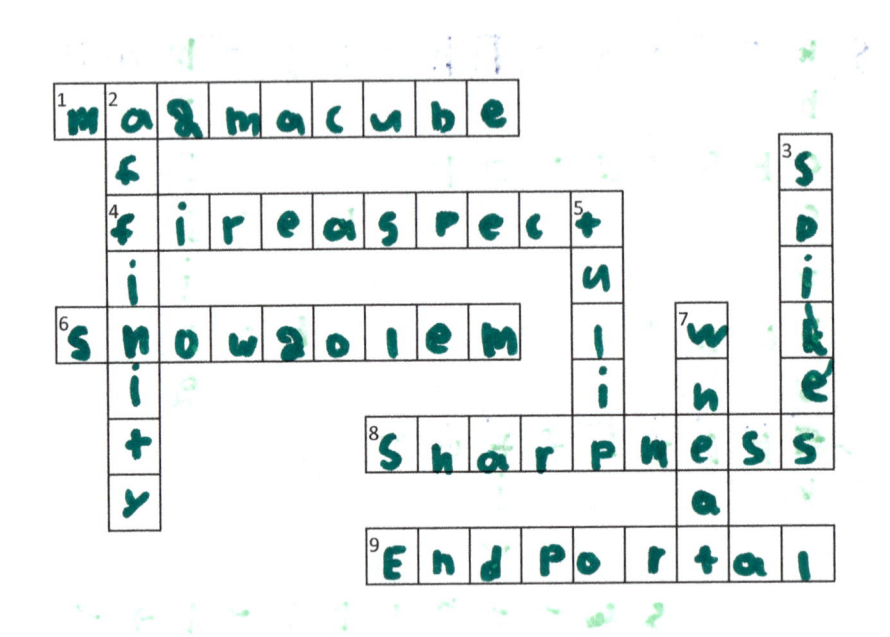

|   | ¹M | ²A | G | M | A | C | U | B | E |   |   |   |   |
|   |   | F  |   |   |   |   |   |   |   |   | ³S |   |
|   | ⁴F | I  | R | E | A | S | P | E | C | T |  I |   |
|   |   | F  |   |   | ⁵ |   |   |   |   |   | P |   |
| ⁶S | N | O | W | G | O | L | E | M |   | ⁷W | I |   |
|   |   | I |   |   | L |   |   |   |   | H | K |   |
|   |   | T |   |   | I |   |   |   |   | E |   |   |
|   |   |   |   |   | ⁸S | H | A | R | P | N | E | S | S |
|   |   | Y |   |   |   |   |   |   |   | A |   |
|   |   |   |   | ⁹E | N | D | P | O | R | T | A | L |

### Across
1. What hostile Nether mob is similar to a slime? (5,4)
4. What enchantment sets an enemy on fire? (4,6)
6. What utility mob do you create using two snow blocks and a pumpkin? (4,5)
8. What enchantment increases the damage dealt in a melee battle? (9)
9. What struture, found in strongholds, is used to travel to The End? (3,6)

### Down
2. Fill in the blanks: An enchantment which increases your mining rate underwater is called Aqua **affinity** (8)
3. Fill in the blanks: A very snowy biome where you may find rabbits, polar bears and strays is called Ice **spikes** (6)
5. Write in the name of a red flower which is good for making rose red dye. (5)
7. What food item is good for crafting bread, cake and cookies? (5)

# 15 Crossword

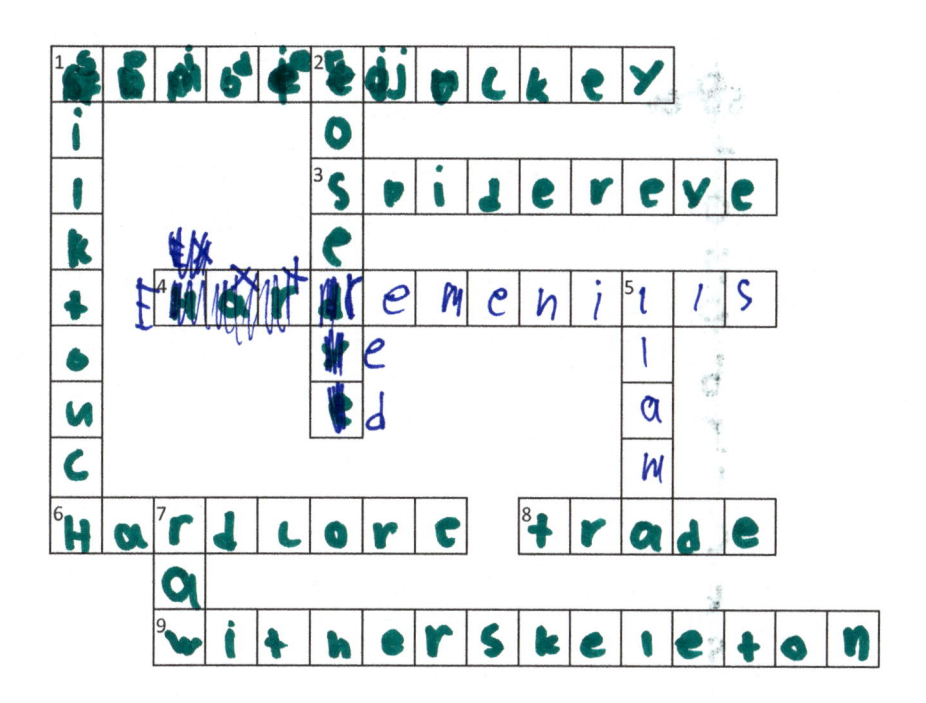

## Across
1 Undead spider rider (6,6)
3 Poisonous food which can be fermented by combining with brown mushroom and sugar (6,3)
4 Mountainous biome where you might find llamas spawning naturally (7,5)
6 Much more difficult variant of survival mode (8)
8 Something you might do with a villager which probably involves emeralds (5)
9 Undead hostile mob which spawns in Nether fortresses (6,8)

## Down
1 Enchantment which causes blocks which you mine to drop themselves instead of the usual items (4,5)
2 A dye you can craft using poppies, red tulips or beetroot (4,3)
5 Neutral mob which can be tamed, looks a bit like a cross between a horse and a sheep (5)
7 Food which isn't cooked (3)

# 16 Crossword

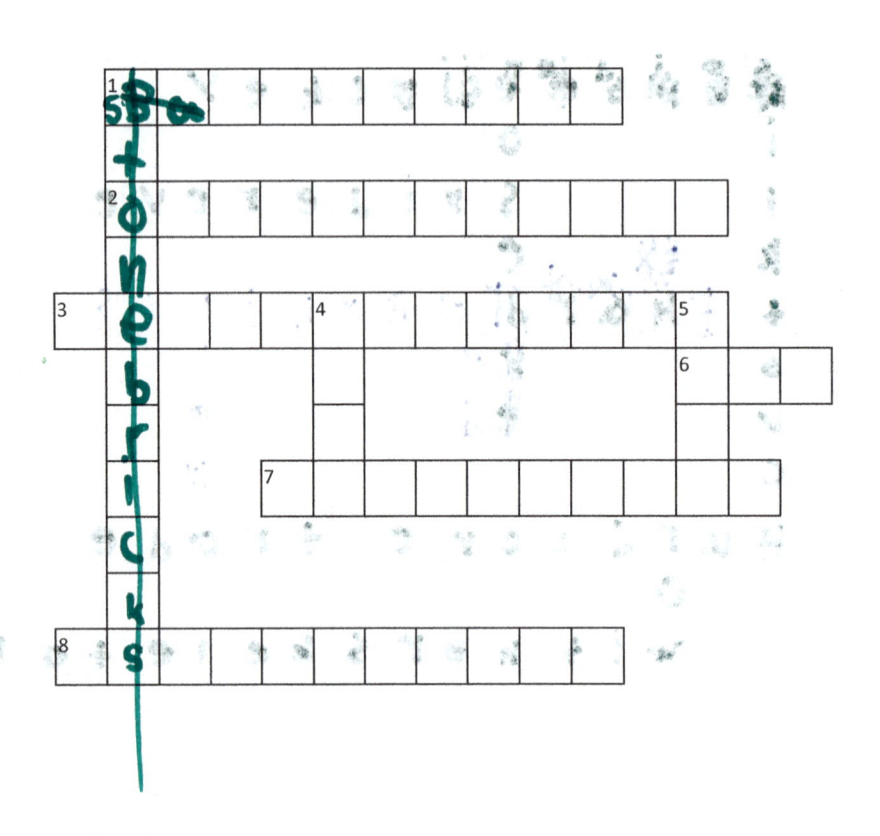

**Across**
1 Eight legged neutral mob with venom (4,6)
2 Red colored liquid food item (8,4)
3 Blaze's fiery attack (5,8)
6 Fill in the blanks: An item for locating end portals is an _ _ _ of Ender (3)
7 Fill in the blanks: an enchantment which increases damage to enemies such as spiders is the Bane of _ _ _ _ _ _ _ _ _ _ (10)
8 Enchantment which gives a player more time to breathe underwater (11)

**Down**
1 A common block used for building, a type of stone (11)
4 The number of gold ingots you need to craft a pair of gold boots (4)
5 An item you can tie to a passive mob so you can keep it tied up (4)

# 17 Numberword

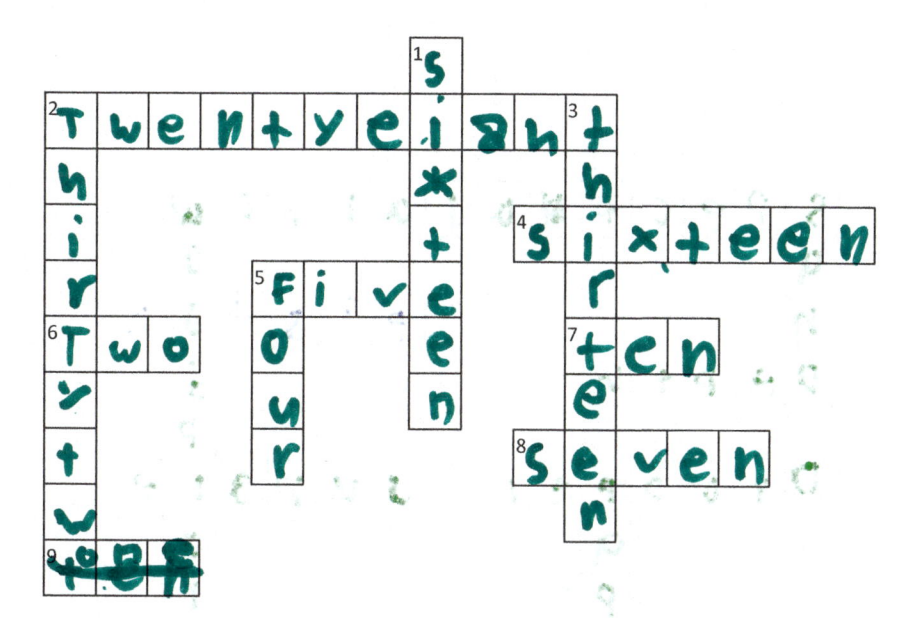

## Across

2. Fill in the blanks: If most items can stack to a maximum of sixty four in one slot, the maximum in two slots of sixty four each is one hundred and twenty eight (6,5)
4. Most items can stack up to sixty four in one slot, but what is a quarter of this? (8)
5. It takes four iron ingots and one redstone to craft one compass, but I want to craft two. I already have two redstone and three iron ingots. How many more iron ingots do I need? (4)
6. It takes two diamonds and a stick to craft a diamond sword. If I have six sticks and four diamonds, how many diamond swords can I craft? (3)
7. If it takes five iron ingots to craft a helmet, how many does it take to craft two? (3)
8. It takes three iron ingots and two wood planks to craft an axe. I have six wood planks and two iron ingots and I want to craft three axes. How many more iron ingots do I need? (5)
9. If it takes seven gold ingots to craft a pair of gold leggings and I have already got thirteen gold ingots, how many pairs of gold leggings can I craft? (3)

## Down

1. If you need eight gold nuggets to craft a golden carrot, how many do you need to craft two? (7)
2. Most items can stack up to sixty four in one slot, but what is half of this? (6,3)
3. It takes eight diamonds to craft a diamond chestplate. I want to make two chestplates and I've got three diamonds, so how many more diamonds do I need? (8)
5. If you need three sticks and three string to craft a bow, how many can you craft with twelve sticks and twelve string?

# 18 Crossword

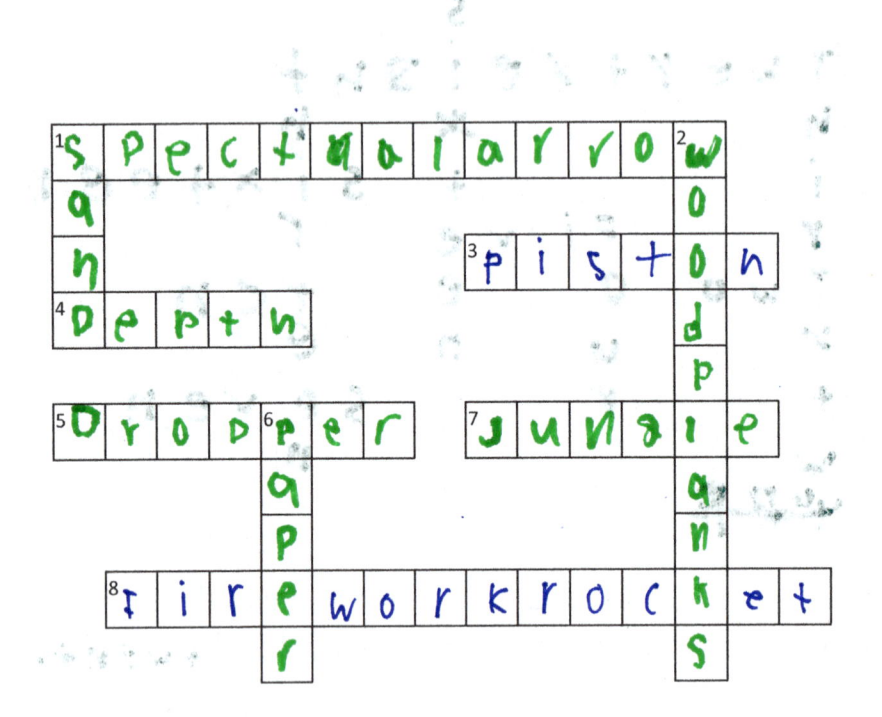

**Across**
1 Type of arrow which produces "glowing" status for 10 seconds (8,5)
3 Block which can be combined with a slimeball to produce a sticky version (6)
4 Fill in the blanks: an enchantment which increases the speed you travel underwater is called  D e p t h  strider (5)
5 Block made from cobblestone and redstone which can be used to eject items (7)
7 Tropical biome where you are likely to find parrots, vines and cocoa pods (6)
8 Exploding item crafted from paper and gunpowder (8,6)

**Down**
1 Block often found in deserts and beaches (4)
2 Common blocks obtained from trees, useful for crafting lots of things, including chests, wood doors and wooden pressure plates (4,6)
6 Item crafted from sugar canes. It's a crafting ingredient for a book (5)

# 19 Crossword

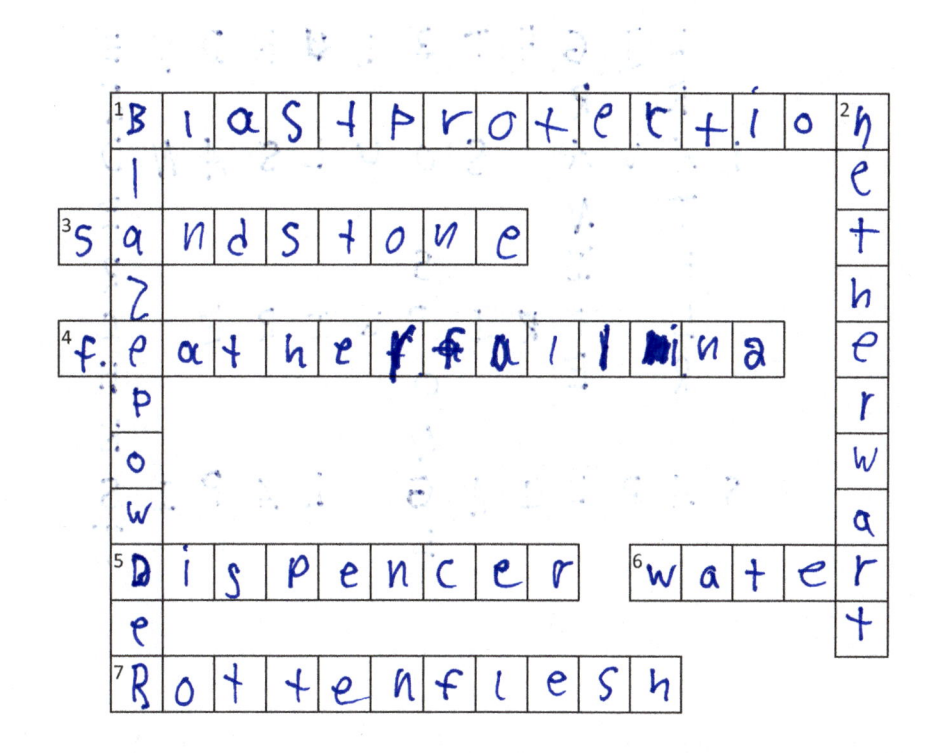

|   | 1B | l | a | s | t | P | r | o | t | e | c | t | i | o | 2n |
|---|---|---|---|---|---|---|---|---|---|---|---|---|---|---|---|
|   | l |   |   |   |   |   |   |   |   |   |   |   |   |   | e |
| 3s | a | n | d | s | t | o | n | e |   |   |   |   |   |   | t |
|   | z |   |   |   |   |   |   |   |   |   |   |   |   |   | h |
| 4f | e | a | t | h | e | r | f | a | l | l | i | n | a |   | e |
|   | p |   |   |   |   |   |   |   |   |   |   |   |   |   | r |
|   | o |   |   |   |   |   |   |   |   |   |   |   |   |   | w |
|   | w |   |   |   |   |   |   |   |   |   |   |   |   |   | a |
|   | 5D | i | s | p | e | n | c | e | r | 6w | a | t | e | r |
|   | e |   |   |   |   |   |   |   |   |   |   |   |   |   | t |
| 7R | o | t | t | e | n | f | l | e | s | h |   |   |   |   |   |

## Across
1. Armor enchantment which reduces damage from explosions (5,10)
3. Solid block which you might find in a desert or a beach (9)
4. This enchantment reduces fall damage (7,7)
5. Block used as a redstone component to dispense items (9)
6. Natural liquid found in oceans, lakes, rivers and springs (5)
7. Food item dropped by zombies which risks food poisoning when you eat it (6,5)

## Down
1. Item crafted from a blaze rod (5,6)
2. Reddish Nether plant which can be used for crafting Red Nether Brick (6,4)

# 20 Crossword

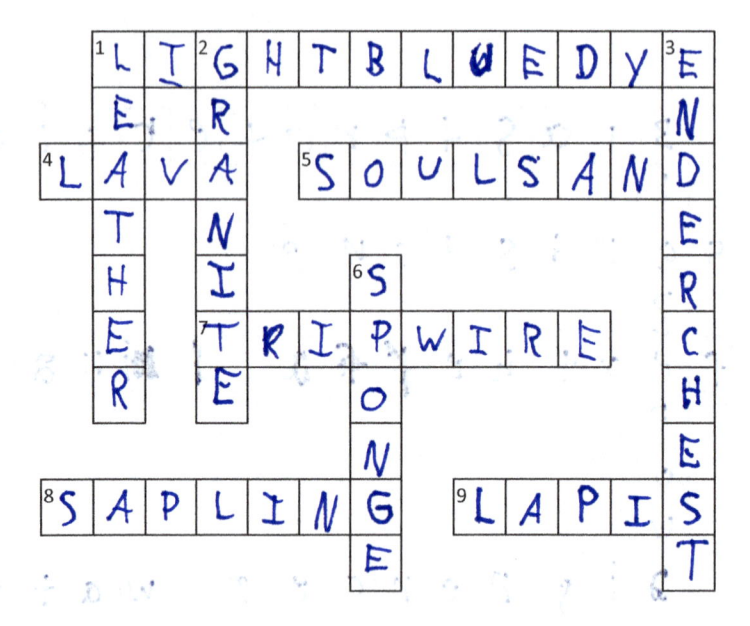

|   | ¹L | I | ²G | H | T | B | L | U | E | D | Y | ³E |   |
|---|----|---|----|---|---|---|---|---|---|---|---|----|---|
|   | E  |   | R  |   |   |   |   |   |   |   |   | N  |   |
| ⁴L| A  | V | A  |   | ⁵S| O | U | L | S | A | N | D  |   |
|   | T  |   | N  |   |   |   |   |   |   |   |   | E  |   |
|   | H  |   | I  |   |   | ⁶S|   |   |   |   |   | R  |   |
|   | E  | ⁷T| R  | I | P | W | I | R | E |   |   | C  |   |
|   | R  | E |    |   |   | O |   |   |   |   |   | H  |   |
|   |    |   |    |   |   | N |   |   |   |   |   | E  |   |
| ⁸S| A  | P | L  | I | N | G |   | ⁹L| A | P | I | S  |   |
|   |    |   |    |   |   | E |   |   |   |   |   | T  |   |

## Across

1. Dye which can be crafted from a blue orchid (5,4,3)
4. Fiery liquid which can produce stone, cobblestone or obsidian when in contact with water (4)
5. Nether block used for growing Nether Wart, which slows movement speed (4,4)
7. What string becomes when it is placed as a block. Can be used in a redstone circuit (8)
8. Small tree (7)
9. Fill in the blanks: A blue decorative mineral block which can be made into dye is called La pis Lazuli (5)

## Down

1. Crafting material obtained from cows, horses and llamas, which can be used to make armor (7)
2. Type of rock which can be mined, or crafted from Diorite and Nether Quartz (7)
3. Special kind of chest which can be crafted using eight Obsidian and one Eye of Ender (5,5)
6. Greenish colored block which can be used to soak up water (6)

# 21 Crossword

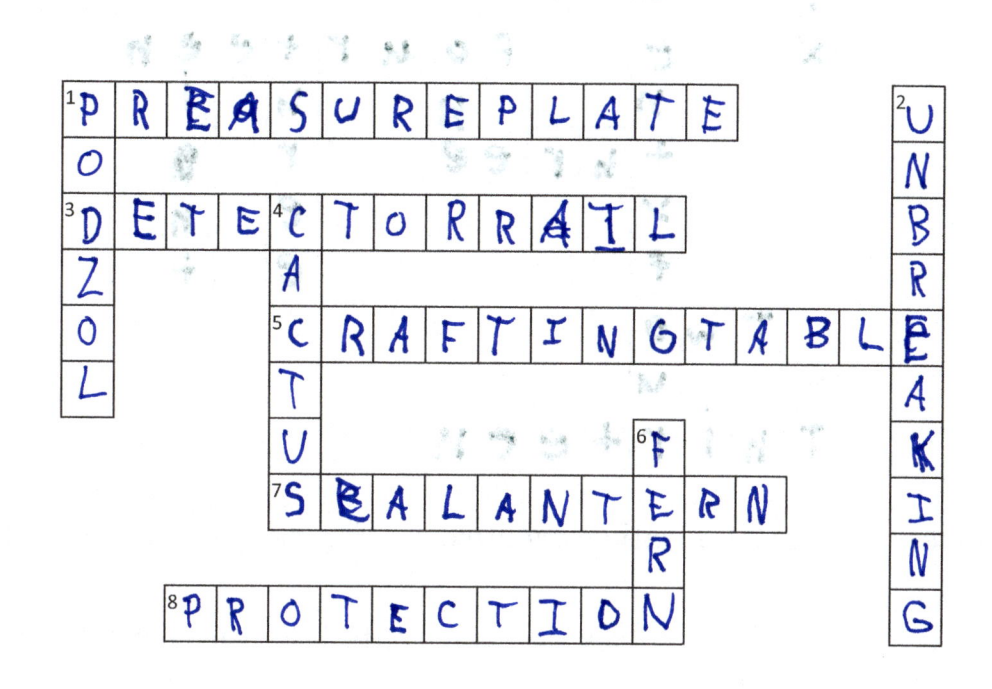

### Across
1 Block which detects when a player, mob, item etc is on top of it; can be light weighted or heavy weighted (8,5)
3 Rail which can detect when minecarts are on it (8,4)
5 Essential for crafting; can itself be crafted from wood planks (8,5)
7 Underwater light source which appears in ocean monuments (3,7)
8 Armor enchantment which reduces damage taken (10)

### Down
1 Dirt-like block which is found on the surface of mega taiga biomes (6)
2 Enchantment which provides increased durability (10)
4 Green prickly plant (5)
6 Green plant which grows naturally in jungle and taiga biomes (4)

# 22 Numberword

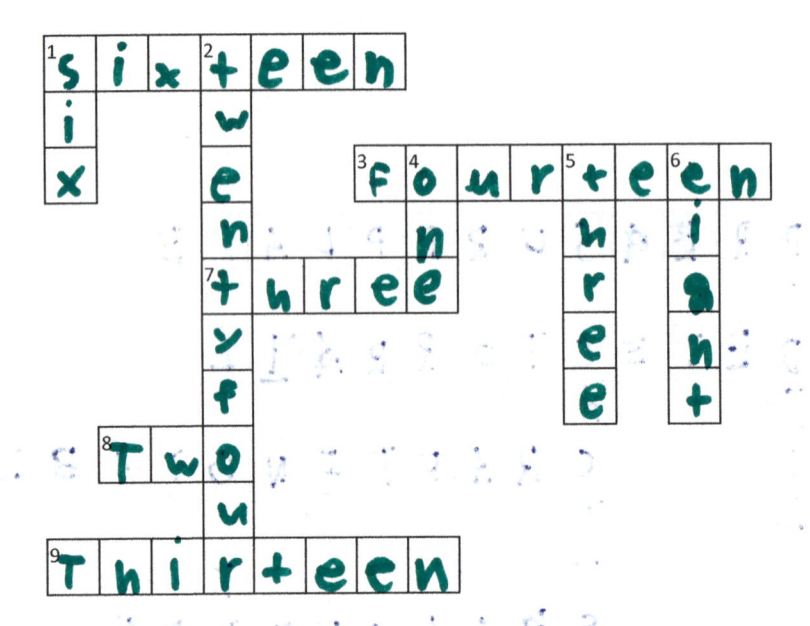

## Across

1. I need eight leather to craft a leather chestplate. How many will I need if I want to craft two? (7)
3. When an iron sword is crafted, it uses two iron ingots. How many iron ingots do I need to craft seven iron swords? (8)
7. I want to make as many diamond axes as I can with lots of sticks and ten diamonds. Each axe uses three diamonds. How many can I make? (5)
8. Crafting a clock takes four gold ingots and one redstone. How many clocks can I craft with twelve gold ingots and two redstone? (3)
9. It takes five iron ingots to craft an iron helmet and a chestplate needs eight ingots. How many do I need to craft both? (8)

## Down

1. It takes three iron ingots and two sticks to craft an iron axe. I want to craft two axes and I've got four sticks but how many iron ingots do I need? (3)
2. It takes eight gold ingots to craft a golden apple. I have plenty of apples. How many ingots do I need to make three golden apples? (6,4)
4. I want two diamond swords. It takes two diamonds to craft a sword and I have three diamonds. How many more diamonds do I need? (3)
5. I have twelve diamonds which I want to make into boots. It takes four diamonds to make each pair of boots. How many pairs can I make? (5)
6. One blaze rod can be crafted into two blaze powder. How many blaze rods do I need to produce sixteen blaze powder? (5)

# 23 Crossword

```
       ¹B O O K S H E L ²F
        E               E
  ³C O L D B E A C H    R
        R               M
        O               E
        C     ⁴L E A ⁵P I N G
  ⁶H U S K     U   N     T
              ⁷C A V E   E
              K   I      D
                  L
```

## Across

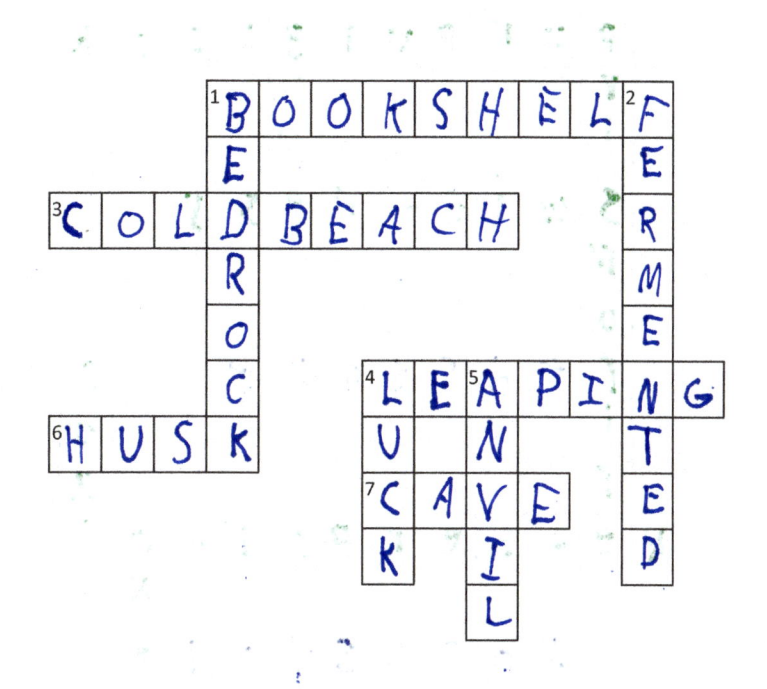

1 Item crafted from wood planks and books, and found in village libraries, which enhances enchanting (9)
3 Sandy biome where snow covers the sand (4,5)
5 Fill in the blanks: the name of a potion which lets a player jump higher and reduce fall damage is a Potion of _leaping_ (7)
6 Taller version of a regular zombie, with an extra-raspy voice (4)
7 Common underground structure (4)

## Down

1 Indestructible block found at the bottom 5 layers of the overworld (7)
2 Fill in the blanks: a useful brewing ingredient for potions such as weakness and harming is called _fermented_ spider eye (9)
4 Status effect which increases a player's chance of high quality loot; this is also the name of a potion (4)
5 Block which you can use to repair items (5)

# 24 Quizword

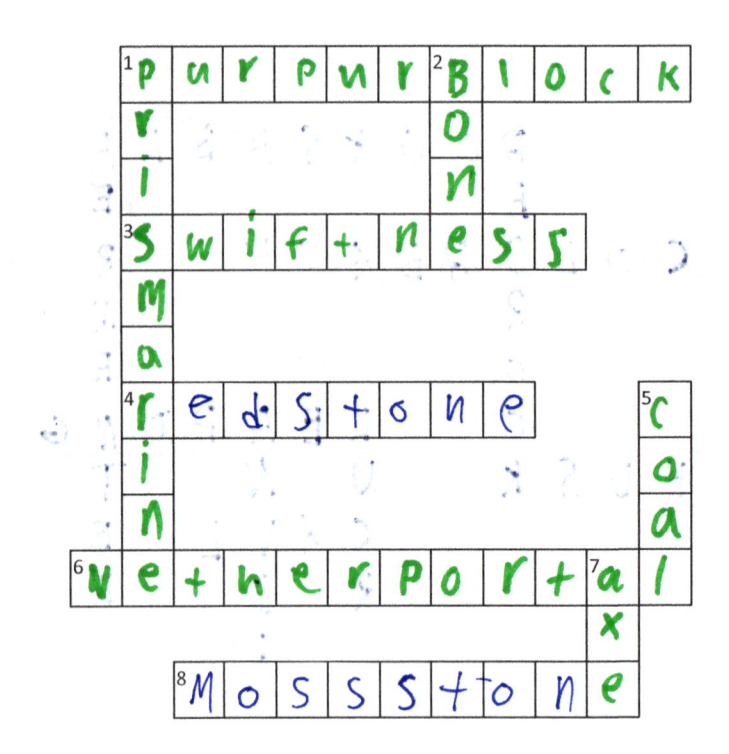

|   |   |   |   |   |   |   |   |   |   |
|---|---|---|---|---|---|---|---|---|---|
| ¹P | u | r | p | u | r | ²B | l | o | c | k |
| r |   |   |   |   |   | o |   |   |   |
| i |   |   |   |   |   | n |   |   |   |
| ³S | w | i | f | t | n | e | s | s |   |
| m |   |   |   |   |   |   |   |   |   |
| a |   |   |   |   |   |   |   |   |   |
| ⁴r | e | d | s | t | o | n | e |   | ⁵C |
| i |   |   |   |   |   |   |   |   | o |
| n |   |   |   |   |   |   |   |   | a |
| ⁶N | e | t | h | e | r | p | o | r | ⁷t | a | l |
|   |   |   |   |   |   |   |   |   | x |
|   |   |   | ⁸M | o | s | s | s | t | o | n | e |

### Across
1 What purple decorative block comes from End Cities? (6,5)
3 Fill in the blanks: What is a potion which increases a player's speed called? Answer: A Potion of swiftness (9)
4 What block can transmit power and be used in circuits? (8)
6 What is a gateway between the Overworld and the Nether called? (6,6)
8 What do you call a block of cobblestone when it has moss growing in its cracks? (4,5)

### Down
1 Which stone-like material is found underwater in ocean monuments? (10)
2 What item is a crafting ingredient for bone meal? (4)
5 What useful block can you use as fuel? (4)
7 What woodcutting tool does a Vindicator use as a weapon? (3)

# 25 Crossword

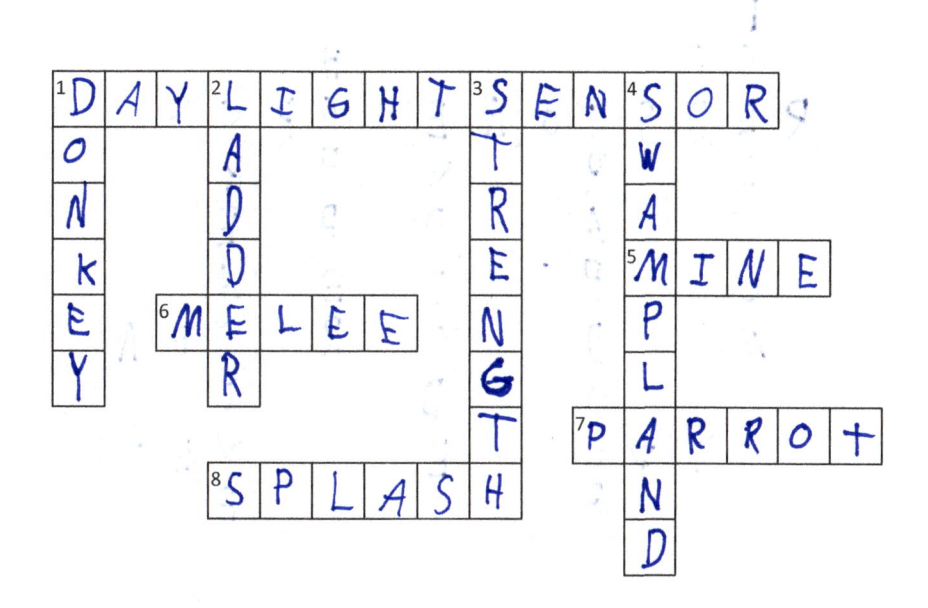

|   | 1D | A | Y | 2L | I | G | H | 3T | S | E | 4N | S | O | R |
|---|---|---|---|---|---|---|---|---|---|---|---|---|---|---|
|   | O |   |   | A |   |   |   | T |   |   | W |   |   |   |
|   | N |   |   | D |   |   |   | R |   |   | A |   |   |   |
|   | K |   |   | D |   |   |   | E |   |   | 5M | I | N | E |
|   | E |   | 6M | E | L | E | E | N |   |   | P |   |   |   |
|   | Y |   |   | R |   |   |   | G |   |   | L |   |   |   |
|   |   |   |   |   |   |   |   | T |   |   | 7P | A | R | R | O | T |
|   |   |   | 8S | P | L | A | S | H |   |   | N |   |   |   |
|   |   |   |   |   |   |   |   |   |   |   | D |   |   |   |

### Across
1 Block which outputs a redstone signal based on whether or not there is any sunlight (8,6)
4 What you do when you dig up blocks with a pickaxe (4)
6 A type of battle at close quarters with weapons such as swords (5)
7 Tameable bird found in Jungle biomes (6)
8 A potion which can be thrown is called a <u>S p l a s h</u> potion (6)

### Down
1 Smaller horse variant with a gray-brown coat and ears which stick up (6)
2 You use this for climbing walls (6)
3 Fill in the blanks: A potion which increases damage in a melee battle is called a Potion of <u>s t r e n g t h</u> (8)
4 Marshy biome with witch huts, mushrooms and sugar canes (9)

# 26 Crossword

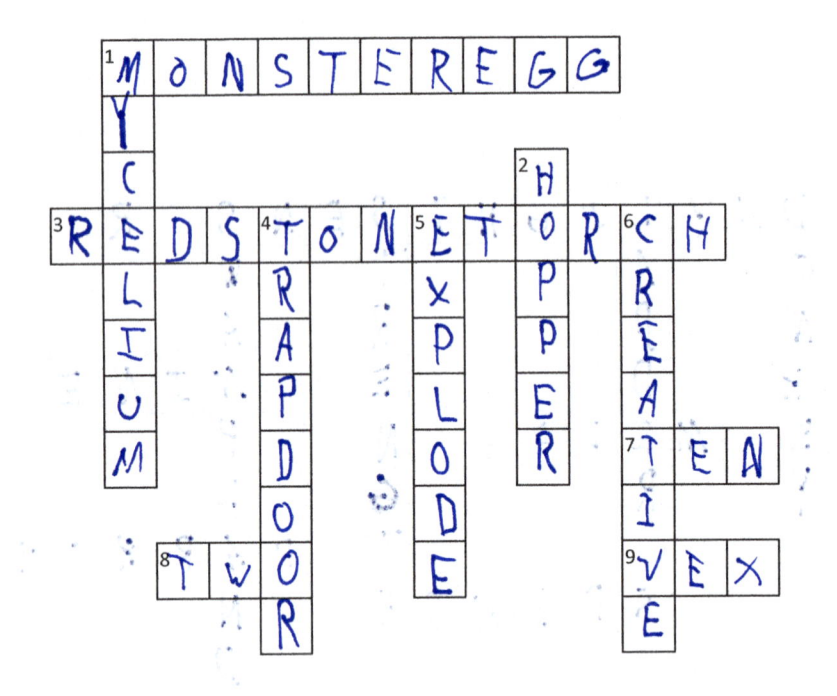

## Across
1. Block which spawns silverfish when broken (7,3)
3. Type of torch crafted from redstone and a stick (8,5)
7. The number of iron ingots you need to craft five iron swords (3)
8. The number of diamonds you need to craft a diamond sword (3)
9. Flying mob which goes around in small groups, and carries an iron sword (3)

## Down
1. Kind of dirt found in mushroom island biomes (8)
2. Container with five slots of inventory space (6)
4. Special kind of door-like block which can be wooden or iron (8)
5. The dangerous thing that creepers and TNT do (5)
6. Minecraft mode where players can fly, have infinite blocks to build with and all mobs are passive (8)

# 27 Crossword

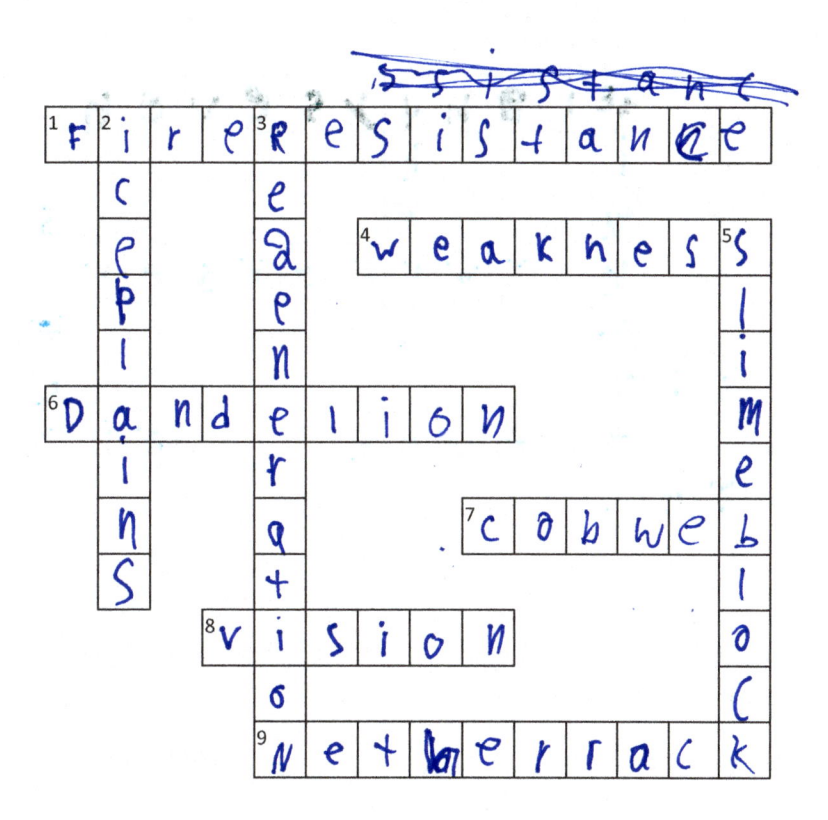

**Across**
1 Potion which makes a player immune to any damage inflicted by heat (4,10)
4 Potion which reduces melee damage (8)
6 Yellow flower that can be used to get rabbits into love mode (9)
7 Block which generates naturally in places like stronghold libraries and abandoned mineshafts. It will slow down the movement of players and mobs, except spiders and cave spiders (6)
8 Fill in the blanks: a potion which brightens everything up to a light level of 15 is a Potion of Night _vision_ (6)
9 Rock-like Nether block which can be smelted to make Nether brick (10)

**Down**
2 Snowy biome with igloos, strays and polar bears (3,6)
3 Potion which restores health (12)
5 Green block which can be crafted from slime balls and which you can bounce up and down on (5,5)

# 28 Numberword

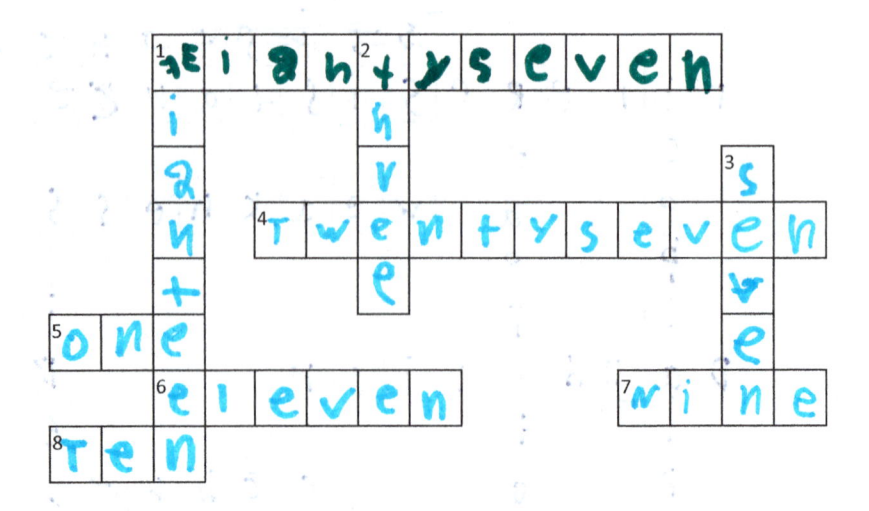

|   |   |   |   |   |   |   |   |   |   |   |
|---|---|---|---|---|---|---|---|---|---|---|
| ¹E | i | g | h | ²t | y | s | e | v | e | n |
| i |   |   |   | h |   |   |   |   |   |   |
| g |   |   |   | v |   |   |   | ³s |   |   |
| h |   |   | ⁴T | w | e | n | t | y | s | e | v | e | n |
| t |   |   |   | e |   |   |   | v |   |   |
| ⁵o | n | e |   |   |   |   |   | e |   |   |
|   |   | ⁶e | l | e | v | e | n |   | ⁷n | i | n | e |
| ⁸T | e | n |   |   |   |   |   |   |   |   |

## Across

**1** If I have a full stack of sixty four items plus twenty three more, how many do I have in total? (6,5)

**4** If I can craft one redstone block into nine redstone, how many redstone can I craft with three redstone blocks? (6,5)

**5** I want to tame four ocelots and I have eleven raw fish. If it takes three raw fish to tame every ocelot, how many more raw fish do I need? (3)

**6** If it takes seven gold ingots to craft golden leggings and four more to craft golden boots, how many do I need to craft both armor items? (6)

**7** I want to tame three wolves. If it takes three bones to tame each wolf, how many bones do I need? (4)

**8** It takes seven cobblestone, a bow and a redstone to craft a dispenser. I want to craft two. I have two bows, two redtsone and four cobblestone. How many more cobblestone do I need? (3)

## Down

**1** If it takes three wheat to craft one loaf of bread, how much wheat do I need to craft six loaves of bread? (8)

**2** Crafting a diamond pickaxe takes two sticks and three diamonds. I have four sticks and three diamonds and want to make two pickaxes. How many more diamonds do I need? (5)

**3** If it takes nine paper to craft one empty map, how many more paper do I need to craft an empty map when I already have two paper? (5)

# 29 Quizword

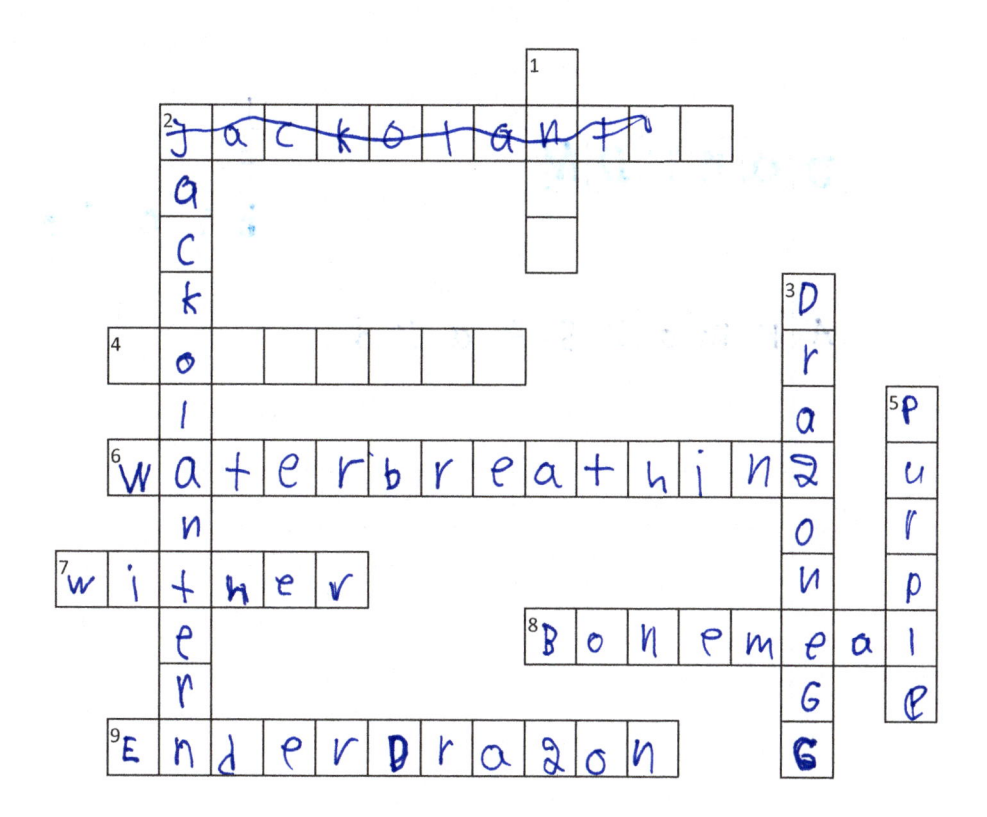

**Across**

2 What is CaptainSparklez' real name? (6,5)

4 What mode do mobs such as pigs and wolves go into when a player encourages them to breed? (4,4)

6 What potion stops the oxygen bar from decreasing when a player is underwater? (5,9)

7 Fill in the blanks: The boss mob which shoots explosive skulls at the player is called The w i t h e r (6)

8 What material crafted from bones is a fertilizer for plants? (4,4)

9 What boss mob activates an exit portal when it is defeated? (5,6)

**Down**

1 Fill in the blanks: the name of a famous Minecraft youtuber is _ _ _ _ Soares Junior (4)

2 What light emitting block can be used to build iron golems and snow golems? (4,1,7)

3 What does the Ender Dragon drop, apart from experience? (6,3)

5 What color is a shulker's shell? (6)

# 30 Crossword

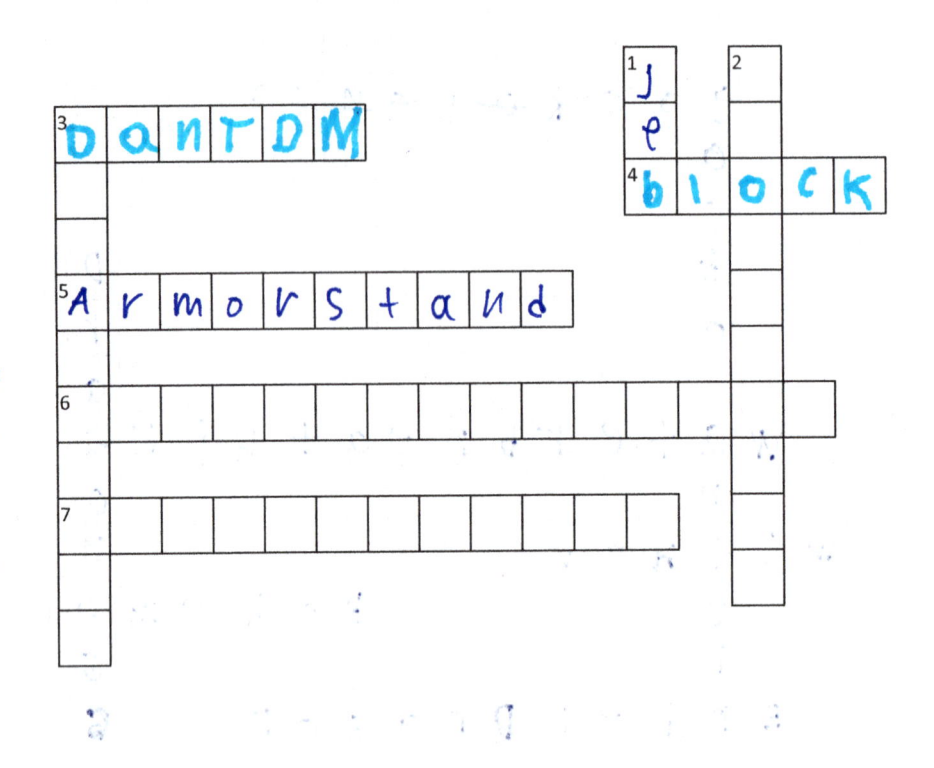

**Across**

3 Minecraft Youtuber whose real name is Daniel Middleton (6)
4 Cube of stuff in Minecraft (5)
5 Something crafted from six sticks and a stone slab, which you can use to show off armor (5,5)
6 Spiky version of a snowy biome with polar bears and rabbits (3,6,6)
7 Potion which makes players impossible to see (12)

**Down**

1 Jens Bergensten's nickname (3)
2 Stony biome which is often found where Extreme Hills biomes meet the ocean (5,5)
3 Measure of the number of times a tool can be used before it will be destroyed (10)

# 31 Crossword

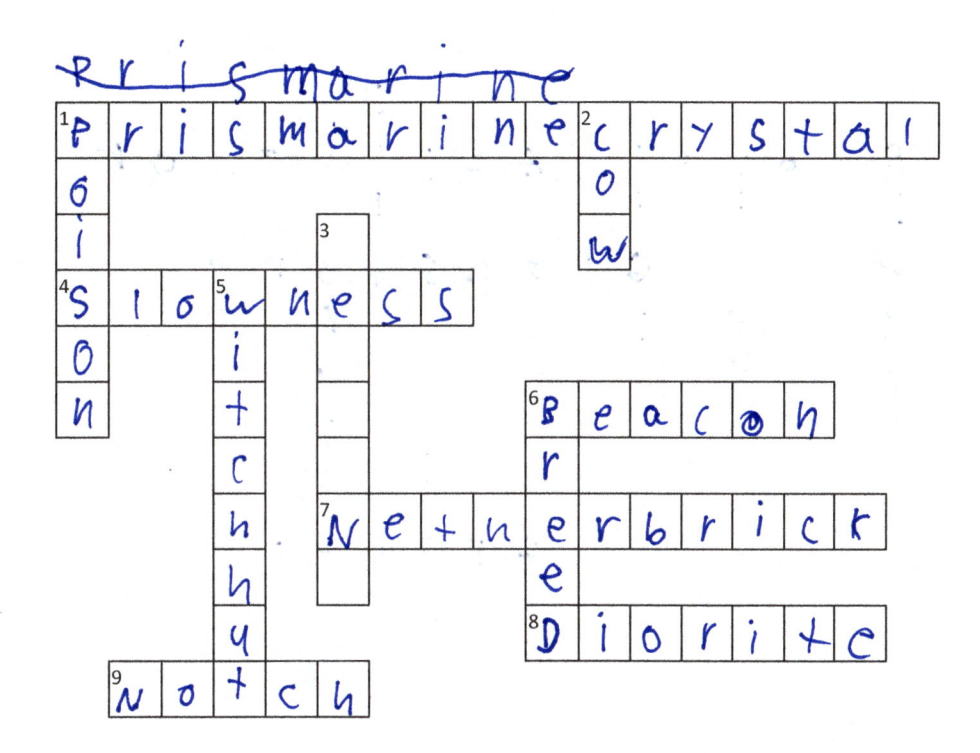

### Across
1. Possible drop from a guardian or elder guardian (10,7)
4. Potion which slows players and mobs (8)
6. Block which produces a light beam (6)
7. Block used to form Nether Fortresses (6,5)
8. Grey rock which can be crafted from nether quartz and cobblestone (7)
9. Nickname of Markus Persson (5)

### Down
1. Potion which causes damage over time (6)
2. What a mooshroom turns into if you shear it (3)
3. Potion which restores 4 health (7)
5. Building found in swamp biomes, which contains an empty cauldron, a crafting table and a flower pot (5,3)
6. What mobs do when they go into love mode (5)

# 32 Crossword

**Across**

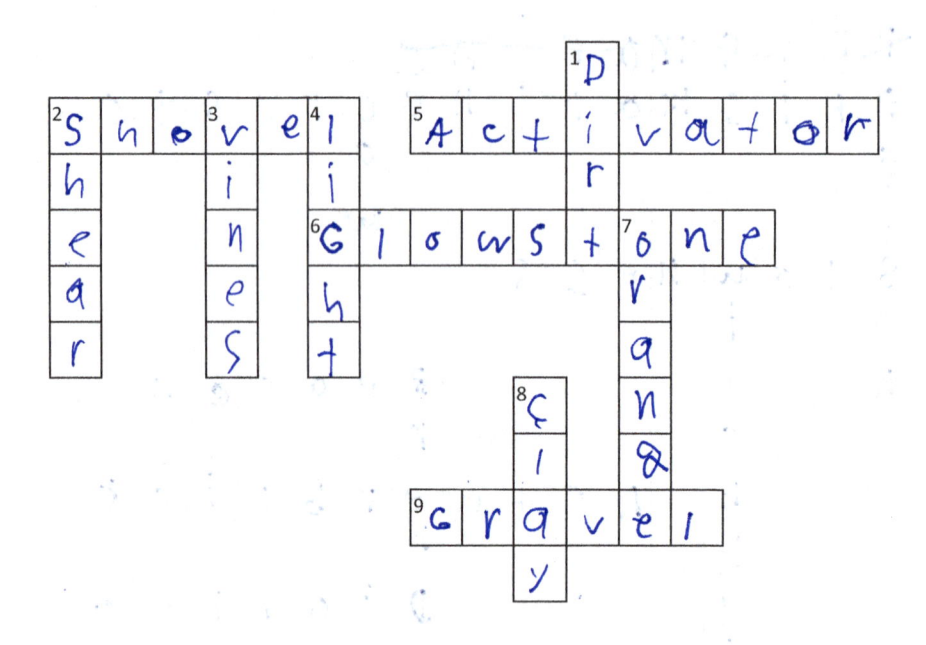

1. Tool used for collecting dirt and other blocks (6)
5. Fill in the blanks: a rail which can "activate" certain minecarts is called an A c t i v a t o r Rail (9)
6. Light-emitting Nether block (9)
9. Block which can be combined with dye and sand to make concrete powder (6)

**Down**

1. Very common block which can be turned into farmland using a hoe (4)
2. Something you can do to a sheep to get wool, or to a mooshroom to get mushrooms (5)
3. Green plants which can be combined with cobblestone to craft moss stone (5)
4. Something which is produced by fire, beacons, torches, and jack'o'lanterns (5)
7. The color of a pumpkin (6)
8. Item which can be smelted to produce bricks (4)

# 33 Numberword

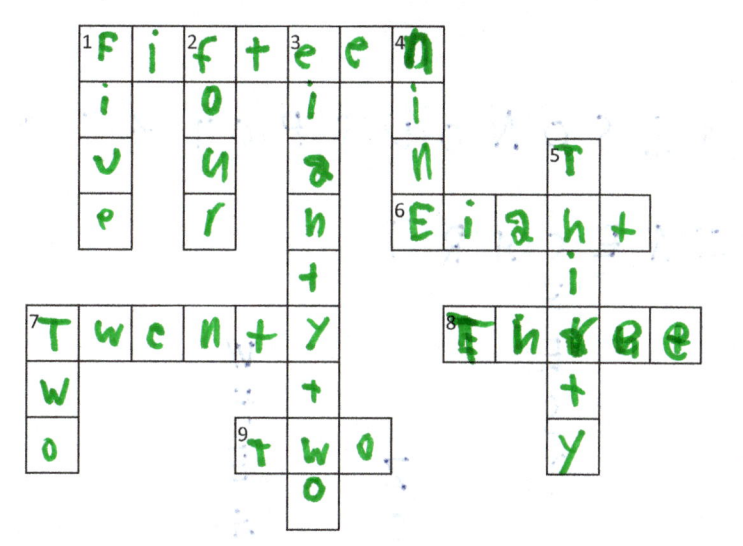

|   | ¹F | i | ²f | t | ³e | e | ⁴n |   |   |
|---|----|---|----|---|----|---|----|---|---|
|   | i  |   | o  |   | i  |   | i  |   |   |
|   | v  |   | u  |   | a  |   | n  |   | ⁵T |
|   | e  |   | r  |   | n  |   | ⁶E | i | g | h | t |
|   |    |   |    |   | t  |   |    |   | i |
| ⁷T | w | e | n | t | y  |   | ⁸T | h | r | e | e |
| w |   |   |   |   | t  |   |    |   | t |
| o |   |   |   | ⁹t | w  | o |    |   | y |
|   |   |   |   |   | o  |   |    |   |   |

## Across

**1** If a mooshroom drops five mushrooms when it's sheared, how many mushrooms are dropped when three mooshrooms are sheared? (7)

**6** It takes five iron ingots to craft a minecart and I want to craft three minecarts. I have seven iron ingots so how many more do I need? (5)

**7** If I need five iron ingots to craft one minecart, how many iron ingots do I need to craft four? (6)

**8** I have loads of milk, eggs and wheat but only five sugar. I want to make four cakes and every cake requires two sugar. How many more sugar do I need? (5)

**9** It takes two iron ingots to craft a pair of shears. I want to craft three pairs of shears but only have four iron ingots. How many more iron ingots do I need? (3)

## Down

**1** I want to craft a diamond chestplate and I have three diamonds. The crafting recipe requires eight diamonds. How many more do I need? (4)

**2** I want to craft two stone swords. Each sword requires two cobblestone so how many cobblestone do I need in total? (4)

**3** Most items stack to a maxiumum of sixty four. If I have a whole stack and eighteen more, how many items do I have in total? (6,3)

**4** If I get three redstone every time I kill a witch, and I kill three witches, how much redstone do I get? (4)

**5** If it takes three gold ingots to craft a golden pickaxe, how many gold ingots do I need for ten golden pickaxes? (6)

**7** If it takes three string and three sticks to craft a bow, how many bows can I craft with seven string and four sticks? (3)

# 34 Crossword

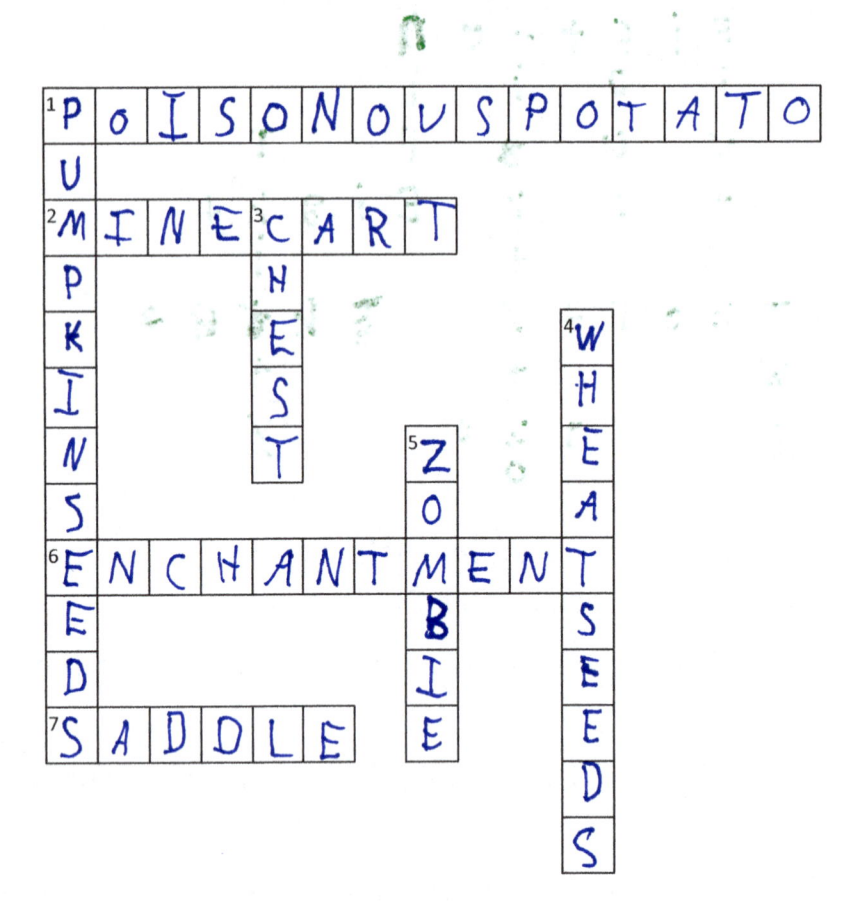

```
 ¹P O I S O N O U S P O T A T O
  U
 ²M I N E ³C A R T
  P     H
  K     E           ⁴W
  I     S            H
  N     T      ⁵Z    E
  S            O     A
 ⁶E N C H A N T M E N T
  E          B     S
  D          I     E
 ⁷S A D D L E E     E
                    D
                    S
```

**Across**

1 Kind of potato which can harm you when you eat it (9,6)

2 Item crafted from 5 iron ingots which can go on rails and can be used to transport things (8)

6 Fill in the blanks: An item which can be crafted from a book, two diamonds and 4 obsidian is called an _ _ _ _ _ _ _ _ _ _ _ table (11)

7 Item you can put on a horse or a pig if you want to ride it (6)

**Down**

1 The type of seeds needed to grow pumpkins (7,5)

3 Block which stores items - a small one has 27 slots of inventory space (5)

4 The kind of seeds you need to grow wheat (5,5)

5 Green hostile mob which catches fire and burns in sunlight (6)

# 35 Quizword

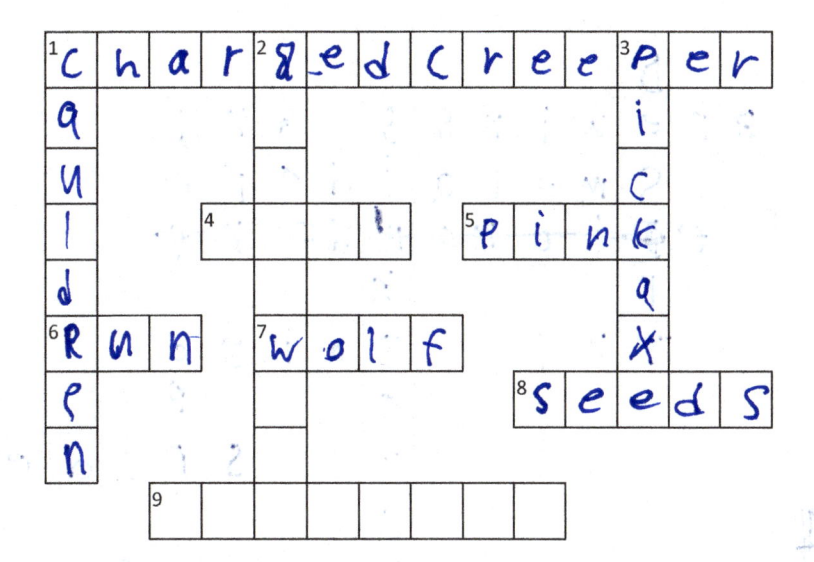

|   | ¹C | h | a | r | ²g | e | d |   | C | r | e | ³e | p | e | r |
|---|---|---|---|---|---|---|---|---|---|---|---|---|---|---|---|
|   | a |   |   |   |   |   |   |   |   |   |   | i |   |   |   |
|   | u |   |   |   |   |   |   |   |   |   |   | c |   |   |   |
|   | l |   |   |   | ⁴ |   |   |   | ⁵P | i | n | k |   |   |   |
|   | d |   |   |   |   |   |   |   |   |   |   | a |   |   |   |
|   | ⁶R | u | n |   | ⁷w | o | l | f |   |   |   | x |   |   |   |
|   | e |   |   |   |   |   |   |   | ⁸s | e | e | d | s |   |   |
|   | n |   |   |   |   |   |   |   |   |   |   |   |   |   |   |
|   |   |   | ⁹ |   |   |   |   |   |   |   |   |   |   |   |   |

### Across

1 What do you get when lightning strikes within 3-4 blocks of a normal creeper? (7,7)

4 What does a llama do to an untamed wolf? (4)

5 What color is a pig? (4)

6 What will a creeper do if it sees an ocelot or a cat? (3)

7 What mob, when tamed, will always try to attack skeletons, wither skeletons and strays? (4)

8 What items can you use to get chickens into love mode? (5)

9 What is the name of a block which is good for planting and growing seeds? (8)

### Down

1 What block, which can hold water, can you craft from 7 iron ingots, or find in a witch hut? (8)

2 What explosive substance can be dropped by creepers, ghasts and witches? (9)

3 What common tool is crafted from two sticks and three of another material, such as iron ingots, diamonds or cobblestone? (7)

# 36 Crossword

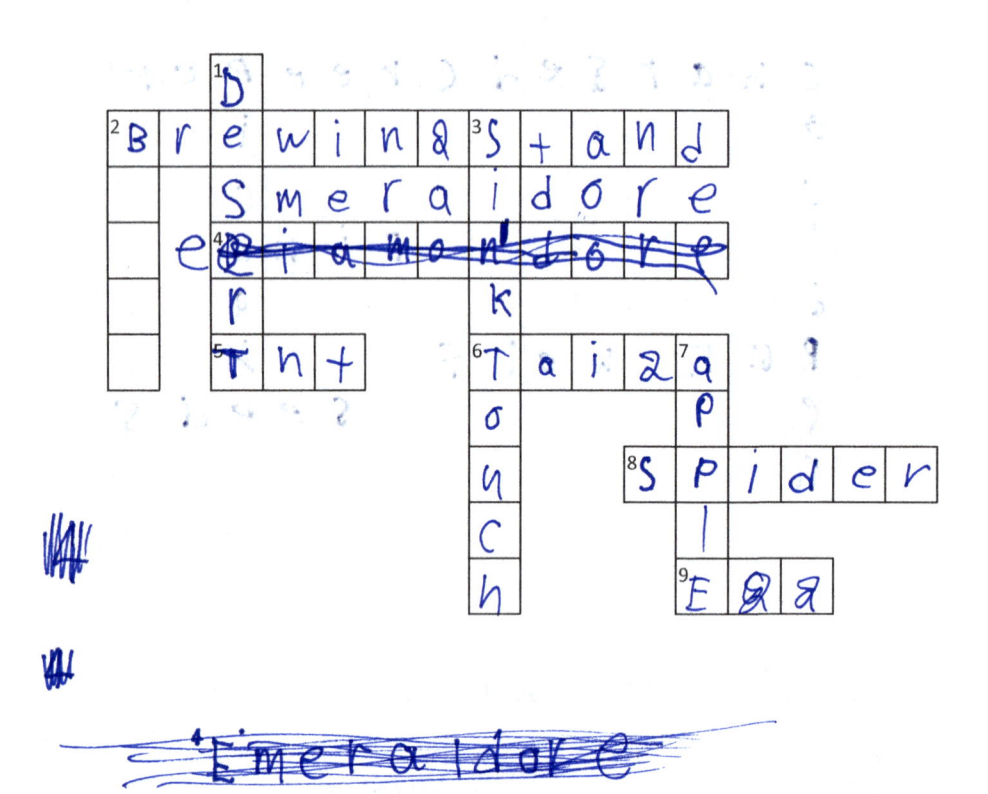

**Across**

2 Block used for brewing potions (7,5)
4 Rarest mineral block in Minecraft, which drops a gemstone when mined (7,3)
5 Explosive block you can craft from four sand and five gunpowder (initials) (3)
6 Fill in the blanks: A biome full of spruce trees, where some trees are extra tall and thick and you can find moss stone boulders, brown mushrooms and podzol is called Mega _ _ _ _ _ (5)
8 Non venomous dark gray arthropod with red eyes (6)
9 Fill in the blanks: An item used to spawn mobs is called a Spawn _ _ _ (3)

**Down**

1 Barren sandy biome with cacti (6)
2 Minecraft region - for instance, taiga, forest or jungle (5)
3 Useful enchantment for pickaxes, axes and shovels (4,5)
7 Food item which is a fruit, can be crafted into a golden or enchanted golden variety (5)

# 37 Crossword

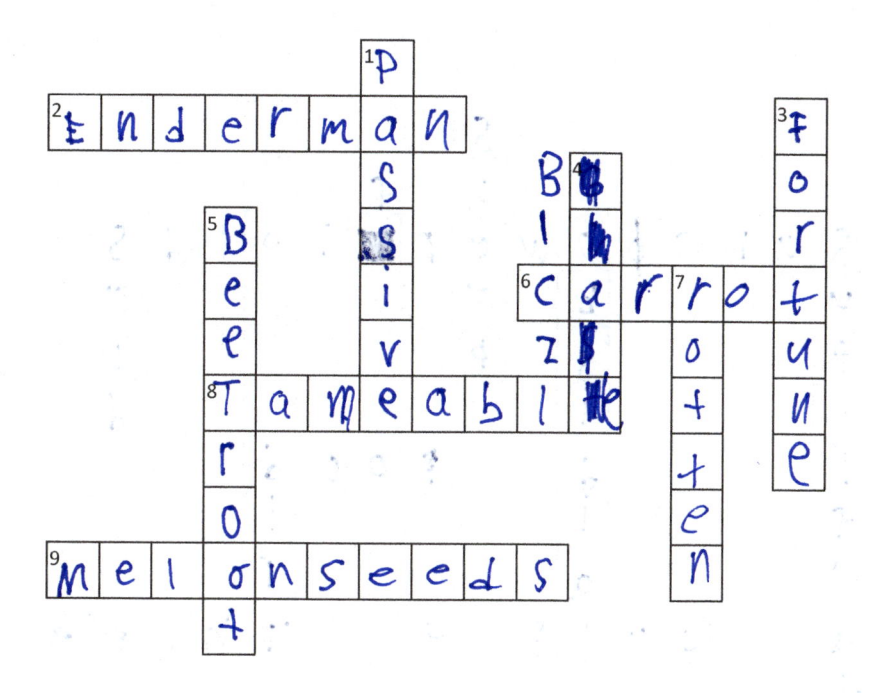

## Across
2 Tall neutral mob which likes to attack endermites (8)
6 Food item which rabbits like to eat (6)
8 Type of mob which includes horses, wolves and ocelots (8)
9 You use these to grow melons (5,5)

## Down
1 Type of mob which doesn't attack players (7)
3 Enchantment which gives a better chance of getting good drops from blocks (7)
4 Hostile Nether mob which can fly and attack with fireballs (5)
5 Food item which can be used to breed pigs (8)
7 Fill in the blanks: A food item dropped by zombies is called rotten flesh (6)

# 38 Crossword

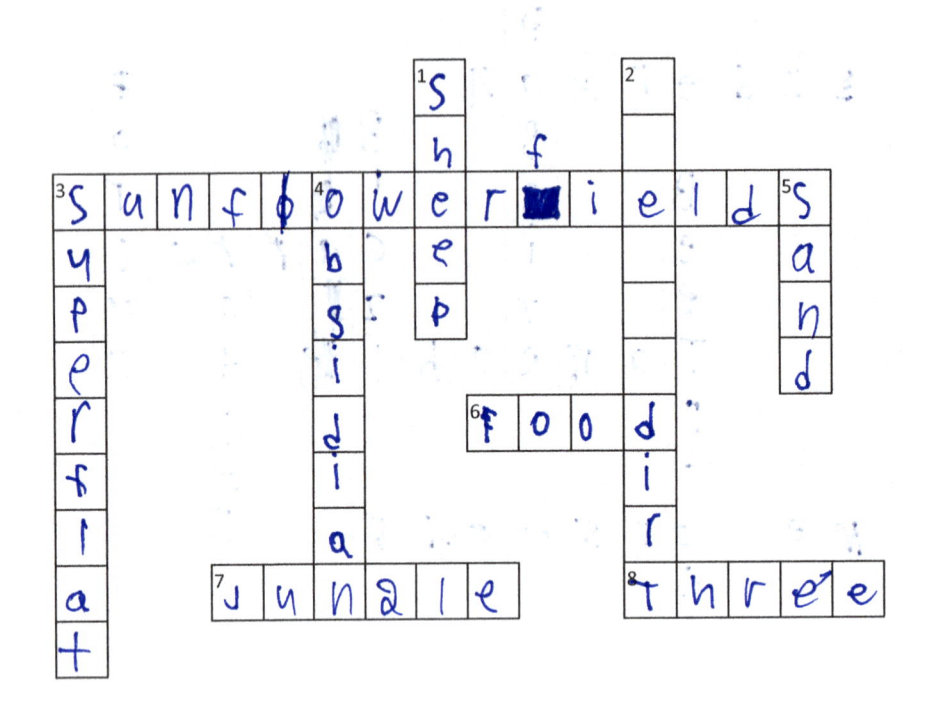

## Across
3 Kind of plains biome full of yellow flowers (9,6)
6 Pumpkin pie, cooked chicken and cookies are all types of this (4)
7 Tropical biome with tall thick trees, vines and parrots (6)
8 The number of diamonds you need to craft a diamond axe (5)

## Down
1 The passive mob which can drop mutton (5)
2 Type of dirt which will not grow grass (6,4)
3 Totally flat world type (9)
4 You get 8 of these when you mine an Ender Chest with a non-enchanted pickaxe (8)
5 A block you can smelt to get glass (4)

# 39 Crossword

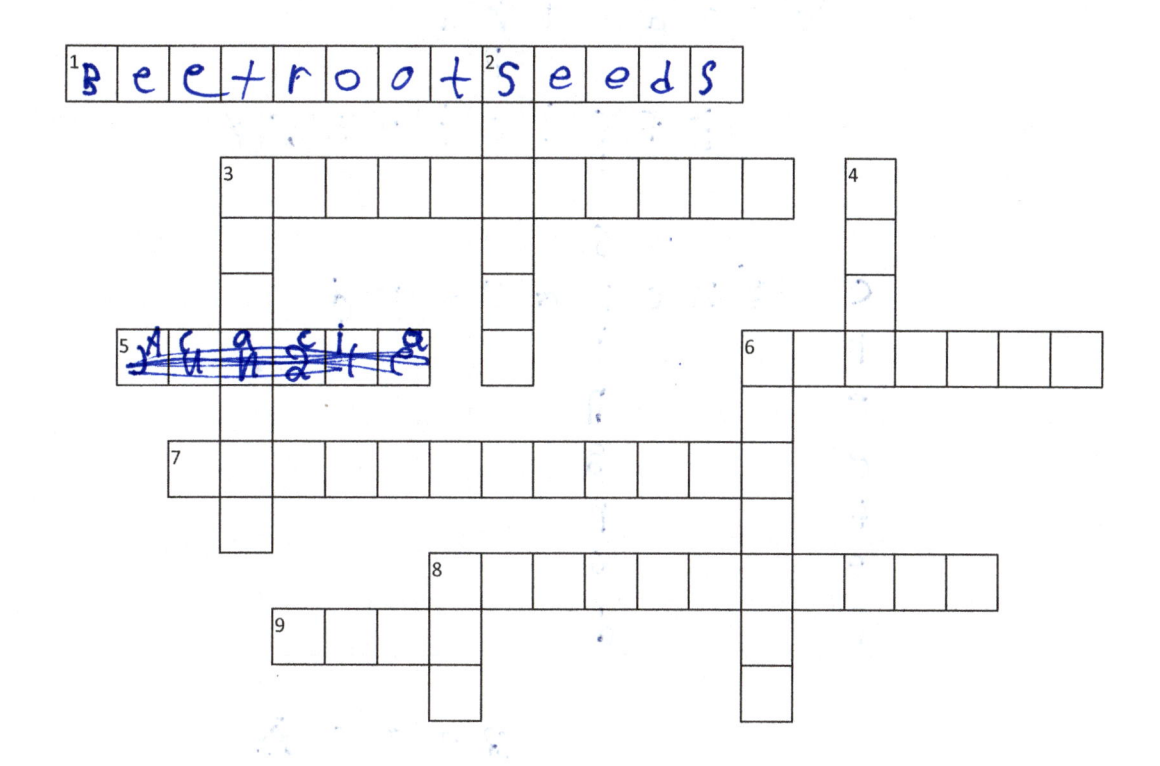

**Across**
1 The seeds you need if you want to grow beetroot (8,5)
3 Type of rail which can increase or decrease the speed of a minecart (7,4)
5 Villager who wears a green robe (6)
6 As well as a flint and a stick, you need one of these to craft four arrows (7)
7 What you get when villagers breed (4,8)
8 Arrow with a potion effect when it hits a mob or player (6,5)
9 Food item you eat from a bowl, which can be mushroom or rabbit variety (4)

**Down**
2 Tool crafted from two iron ingots which you use to get wool from sheep (6)
3 Sloping biome which generates in a mesa or savanna biome (7)
4 Reddish colored biome with red sand where you are more likely to find gold ore (4)
6 Something you need if you want to cook raw beef to make it into steak (7)
8 The number of iron ingots you need to make a heavy weighted pressure plate (3)

# 40 Crossword

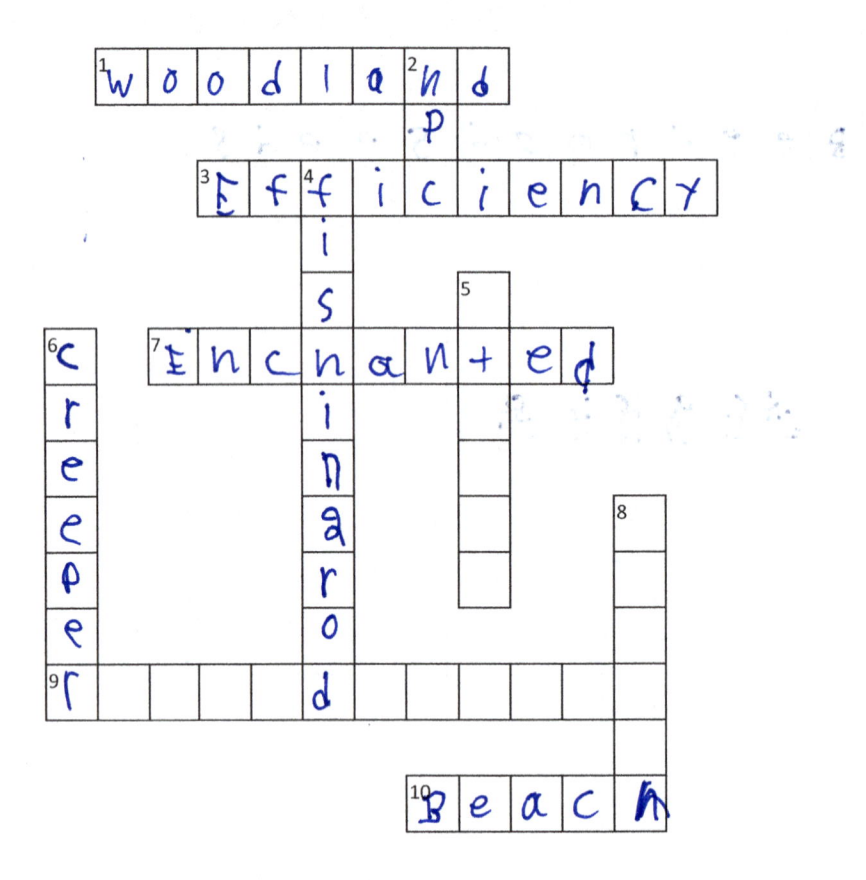

## Across

1 Fill in the blanks: The place where Vindicators and Evokers spawn is called a w o o d l a n d Mansion (8)

3 This enchantment gives an increase in mining speed (10)

7 Fill in the blanks: The item you can craft from an apple and 8 blocks of gold is called an e n c h a n t e d golden apple (9)

9 Biome of dark oak trees. The only biome where illagers and the totem of undying can be found (6,6)

10 Sandy biome where the ocean meets the landscape (5)

## Down

2 Character, such as a villager, who isn't a player (initials) (3)

4 Tool you can craft from three sticks and two string (7,3)

5 Fill in the blanks: YouTuber Joseph Garrett is also known as _ _ _ _ _ _ Cat (6)

6 Common hostile mob which runs away from ocelots and cats (7)

8 What you've got when something strange happens or goes wrong in Minecraft (6)

# 41 Crossword

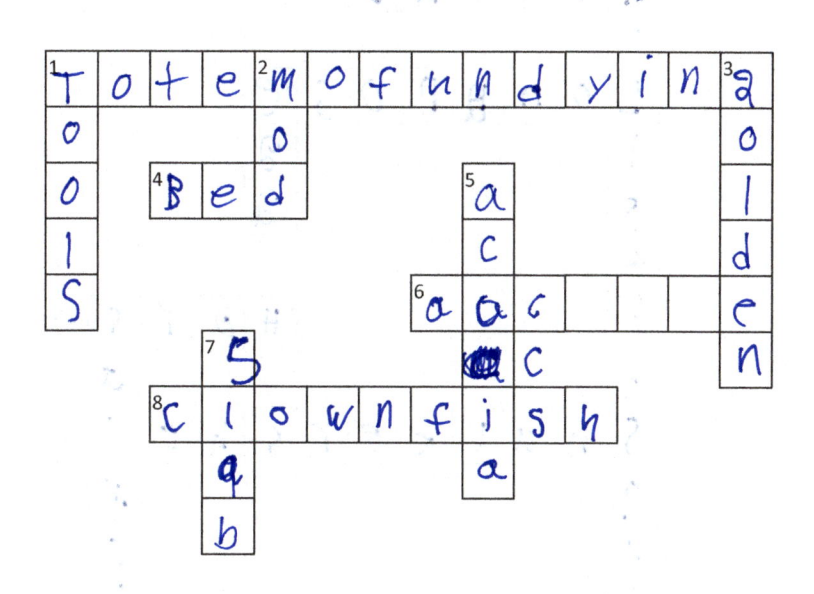

**Across**
1. Drop from an Evoker which can save a player from death (5,2,7)
4. Block a player can sleep in, which allows the player to reset their spawn point (3)
6. What you need to make two llamas breed (3,4)
8. Orange and white striped Minecraft fish (9)

**Down**
1. Shovels, shears, pickaxes and hoes are all types of these (5)
2. Modifications to the Minecraft world (3)
3. The kind of carrot you can use to get tamed horses into love mode (6)
5. Tree found in the savanna biome (6)
7. Half-version of a block (4)

# 42 Crossword

|   | 1 I | r | o | n | i | n | g | o | t |   |   |
|---|---|---|---|---|---|---|---|---|---|---|---|
|   | b |   |   |   |   |   |   |   |   |   |   |
|   | 2 A | l | b | i | n | o |   |   |   |   |   |
|   | l |   |   |   |   |   |   |   |   |   |   |
|   | 3 L | o | n | g | n | o | s | 4 e |   |   |   |
|   | i |   |   |   |   |   |   | g |   |   |   |
|   | s |   |   |   |   |   |   | g |   |   |   |
|   | t |   |   |   |   |   |   |   |   |   |   |
|   | i |   |   |   |   | 5 H | o | r | 6 S | e |   |
|   | c |   |   |   |   |   |   |   | a |   |   |
|   | 7 S | h | u | l | k | e | r | s | h | e | l | l |
|   | q |   |   |   |   |   |   |   | m |   |   |
|   | u |   |   |   |   |   |   |   | o |   |   |
|   | i |   |   |   |   |   |   |   | n |   |   |
|   | 8 D | o | o | r | s |   |   |   |   |   |   |

**Across**

1 Metal crafting ingredient obtained by smelting iron ore (4,5)
2 Rabbit type with white fur and red eyes (6)
3 Fill in the blanks: Stampy Cat's second YouTube channel is called Stampy Longnose (8)
5 Fill in the blanks: The kind of armor which a tameable, rideable mob can wear is called horse armor (5)
7 Drop from a shulker which is a crafting ingredient for a purple shulker box (7,5)
8 You need these to get villagers to breed (5)

**Down**

1 YouTuber who is also known as Squid Nugget (15)
4 Something a chicken lays (3)
6 Type of Minecraft fish (6)

# 43 Crossword

## Across

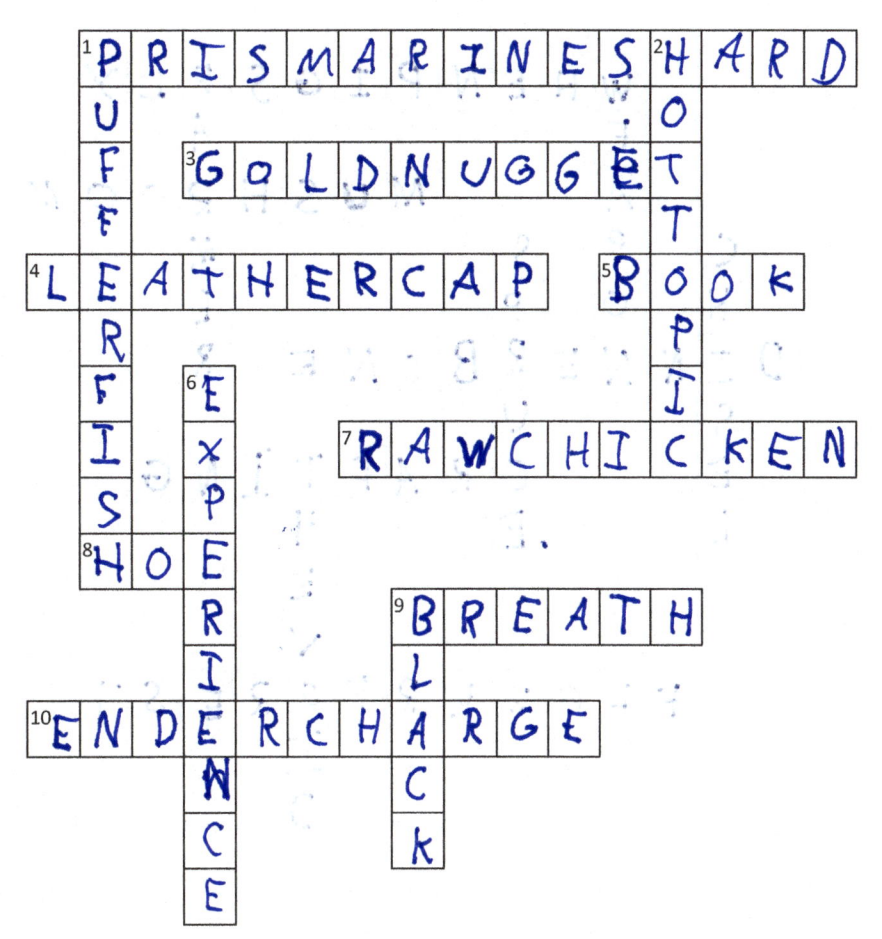

1. Possible Guardian or Elder Guardian drop which can be used to craft dark prismarine or sea lantern (10,5)
3. Common precious metal drop from a zombie pigman (4,6)
4. Type of helmet made of leather (7,3)
5. Item you can craft from three paper and one leather (4)
7. Food item dropped by a passive mob that lays eggs (3,7)
8. Tool used to till earth, turning dirt or grass into farmland (3)
9. Fill in the blanks: Ingredient for a lingering potion, obtained using a glass bottle near the Ender Dragon's breath attack is called Dragon's breath (6)
10. The name of the Ender Dragon's special fireball attack (5,6)

## Down

1. Type of poisonous Minecraft fish (10)
2. Achievement for constructing a furnace out of eight stone blocks (3,5)
6. You get 50 of this for killing The Wither, and 12,000 for the Ender Dragon (10)
9. The color of obsidian (5)

# 44 Crossword

```
    W H E N P I G S F L Y
    E               A
    A       M U S H R O O M
  C P   S           M
  H O   P           E
  D I N N E R B O N E
  I S   R           R
  S U
  E   C R A F T I N G
  L   E     H
            E
            V
  F L O W E R F O R E S T
            I
            D
```

**Across**

1 Achievement obtained by riding a saddled pig off a cliff (4,4,3)
3 Stew ingredient which can be red or brown (8)
6 The name you can put on a mob's nametag to make it flip upside down (10)
7 The method by which players make things in Minecraft (8)
9 Forest biome with nearly every flower and tall plant in the game (6,6)

**Down**

1 Swords, bows and axes are all types of these (6)
2 Profession of a villager with a brown robe (6)
4 Popular Minecraft mod which introduces a huge number of new decorative blocks to the game (6)
5 Type of Minecraft tree mainly found in the Taiga biome (6)
8 The empty space below layer zero in any Minecraft dimension (3,4)

# 45 Quizword

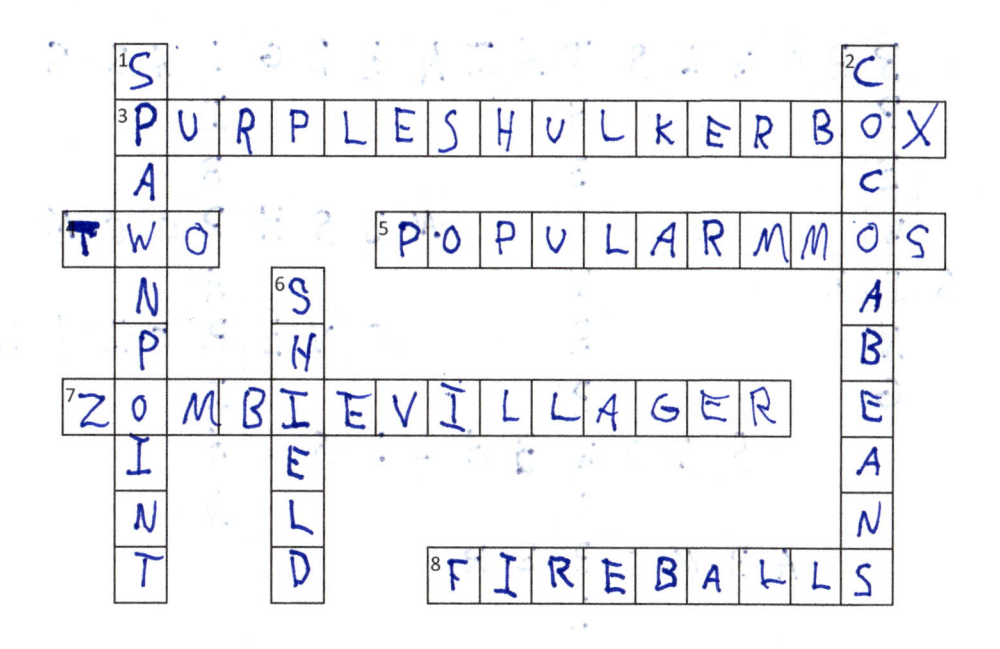

|   | ¹S |   |   |   |   |   |   |   |   | ²C |   |
|---|---|---|---|---|---|---|---|---|---|---|---|
|   | ³P | U | R | P | L | E | S | H | U | L | K | E | R | B | O | X |
|   | A |   |   |   |   |   |   |   |   | C |   |
| ⁴T | W | O |   |   | ⁵P | O | P | U | L | A | R | M | M | O | S |
|   | N |   |   | ⁶S |   |   |   |   |   | A |   |
|   | P |   |   | H |   |   |   |   |   | B |   |
| ⁷Z | O | M | B | I | E | V | I | L | L | A | G | E | R |
|   | I |   |   | E |   |   |   |   |   | A |   |
|   | N |   |   | L |   |   |   |   |   | N |   |
|   | T |   |   | D |   | ⁸F | I | R | E | B | A | L | L | S |

## Across

**3** What item, crafted from two shulker shells and a chest, is useful for for storage and transportation? (6,7,3)

**4** What is the maximum number of glowstone dust that a Blaze normally drops on death? (3)

**5** What YouTuber has the real name Patrick Julianelle? (11)

**7** What might you get if a zombie kills a villager? (6,8)

**8** What explosive items do Ghasts shoot at players? (9)

## Down

**1** What is the place where a player respawns called? (5,5)

**2** What crop do you harvest from cocoa plants? (5,5)

**6** What item can you craft from six wood planks and an iron ingot and use to protect yourself in battle? (6)

# 46 Crossword

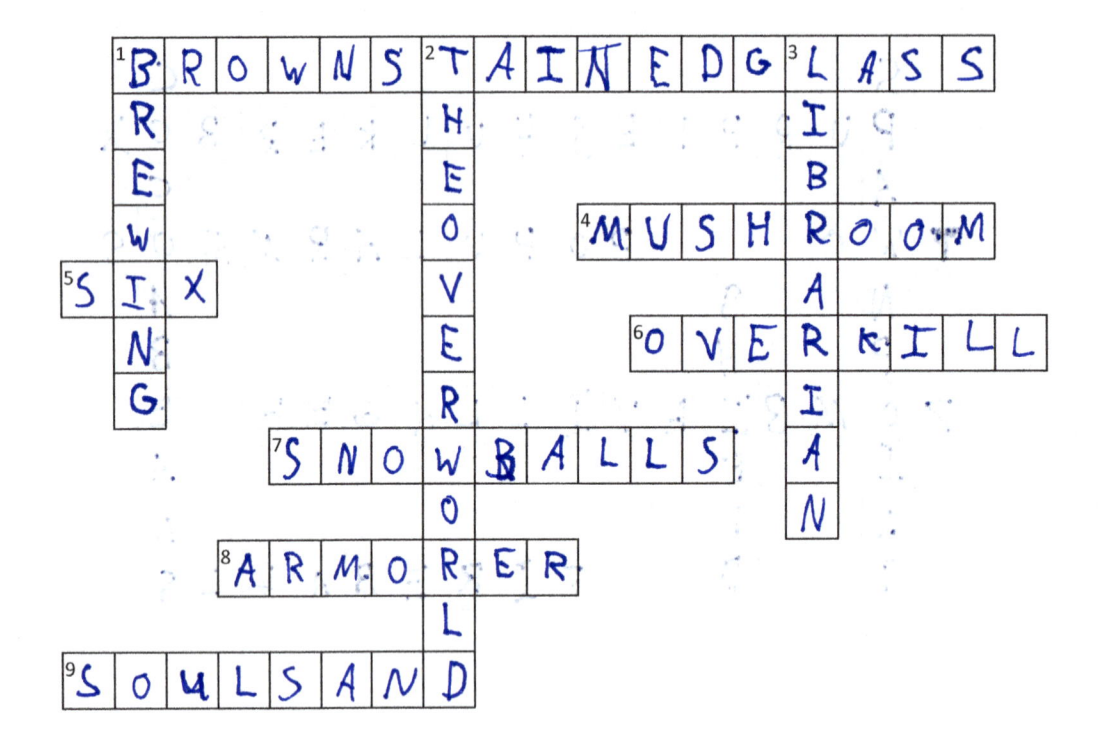

|   |   | ¹B | R | O | W | N | ²S | T | A | I | N | E | D | G | ³L | A | S | S |
|---|---|---|---|---|---|---|---|---|---|---|---|---|---|---|---|---|---|---|
|   |   | R |   |   |   |   | H |   |   |   |   |   |   |   | I |   |   |   |
|   |   | E |   |   |   |   | E |   |   |   |   |   |   |   | B |   |   |   |
|   |   | W |   |   |   |   | O |   |   |   | ⁴M | U | S | H | R | O | O | M |
| ⁵S | I | X |   |   |   |   | V |   |   |   |   |   |   |   | A |   |   |   |
| I |   |   |   |   |   |   | E |   |   |   | ⁶O | V | E | R | K | I | L | L |
| N |   |   |   |   |   |   | R |   |   |   |   |   |   |   | I |   |   |   |
| G |   |   |   |   | ⁷S | N | O | W | B | A | L | L | S |   | A |   |   |   |
|   |   |   |   |   |   |   |   |   | O |   |   |   |   |   | N |   |   |   |
|   |   |   |   | ⁸A | R | M | O | R | E | R |   |   |   |   |   |   |   |   |
|   |   |   |   |   |   |   |   |   | L |   |   |   |   |   |   |   |   |   |
| ⁹S | O | U | L | S | A | N | D |   |   |   |   |   |   |   |   |   |   |   |

**Across**

1 The type of glass you can craft from glass and cocoa beans (5,7,5)
4 Fill in the blanks: A rare biome with mooshrooms, and mycelium instead of grass on its surface is called M U S H R O O M Island (8)
5 The number of diamonds you need to make three diamond swords (3)
6 Achievement obtained by dealing nine hearts of damage in one hit (8)
7 Throwable items which can be obtained from breaking snow blocks (9)
8 Type of blacksmith villager who makes armor (7)
9 Block which makes players and mobs go slower, and can suffocate endermites and silverfish (4,4)

**Down**

1 The process of creating potions (7)
2 The name of the dimension where players start in Minecraft (3,9)
3 Villager who likes books (9)

# 47 Quizword

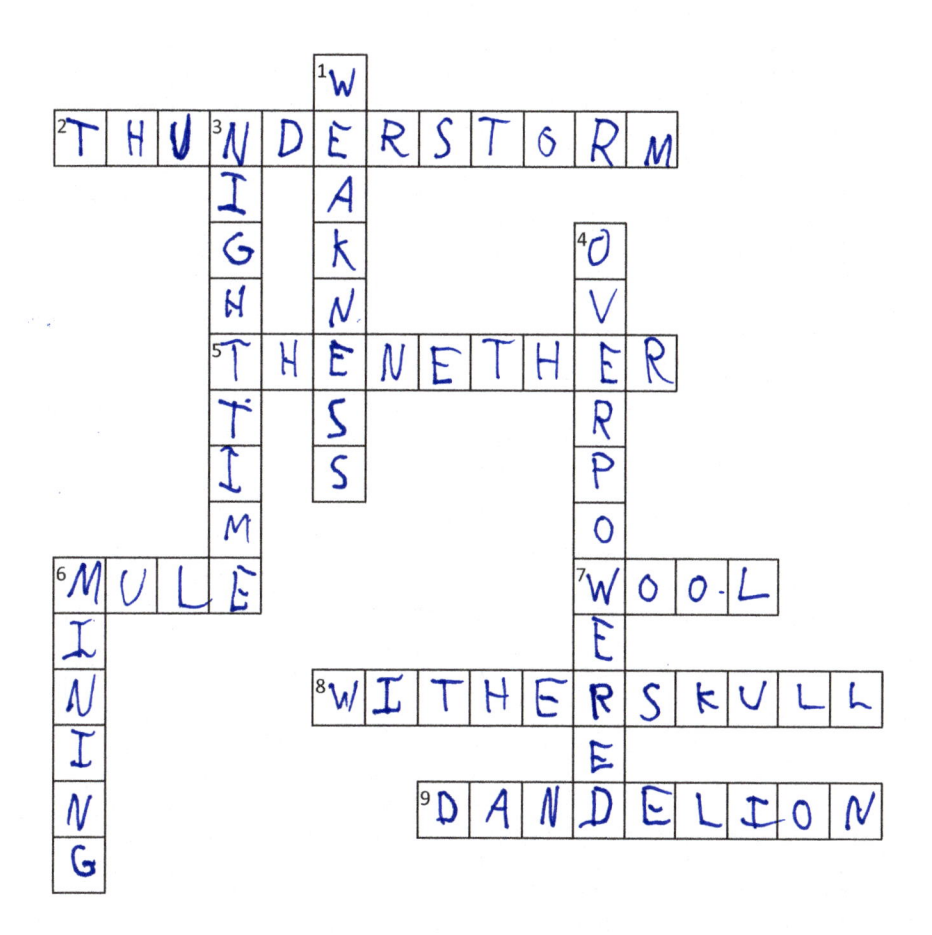

### Across
2 During what weather condition in Minecraft do lightning strikes occur? (12)
5 What is the name of Minecraft's fiery, lava-filled dimension? (3,6)
6 Which horse variant, as well as a donkey, can carry a chest? (4)
7 Which block can be harvested by using shears on a sheep? (4)
8 What explosive thing does The Wither shoot at players to attack them? (6,5)
9 Fill in the blanks: A yellow dye in Minecraft is called dandelion Yellow (9)

### Down
1 What splash potion do you need to put on a zombie villager, before feeding it a golden apple, to turn it into a villager? (8)
3 What's it called at the time of the day/night cycle when everything goes dark? (9)
4 What achievement do you get for eating an enchanted golden apple? (11)
6 What is a common way of obtaining blocks in Minecraft? (7)

# 48 Crossword

**Across**

1 Drop from a pig which has been killed while it's on fire (6,8)
3 Things that Endermen like to pick up and move around (6)
6 What a player usually does when he steps in lava (3)
7 Icy river biome (6,5)
8 What dirt turns into when you use a hoe on it (8)
9 Achievement you obtain by killing a hostile mob (7,6)
10 A kind of "crafting" you do in a furnace (8)

**Down**

1 Food item which will kill a parrot if you feed it to the mob (6)
2 Crafting ingredient for End Rods (6,6,5)
3 The color of a Minecraft bat (5)
4 The number of sticks you would need to craft five shovels (3)
5 Achievement you obtain by turning wheat into bread (4,5)

# 49 Numberword

*[Completed crossword grid with answers filled in:]*

- 1 Across: TWENTYFIVE
- 5 Across: TWO
- 6 Across: SIXTEEN
- 7 Across: SEVEN
- 1 Down: THIRTYFIVE
- 2 Down: EIGHT
- 3 Down: FOUR
- 4 Down: EIGHTEEN
- 5 Down: TWELVE

## Across

**1** If a ghast drops five experience when killed, how much experience do five ghasts drop? (6,4)

**5** It takes four iron ingots and one redstone to craft a compass. If I have nine iron ingots and three redstone, how many compasses can I make? (3)

**6** If a villager will pay one emerald for every eight melons a player sells, how many melons do you need to sell to get two emeralds? (7)

**7** If it takes fourteen diamonds to make two pairs of diamond leggings, how many diamonds does it take to make one pair? (5)

## Down

**1** If an iron golem drops three to five iron ingots when it dies, what's the maximum number of ingots you can get from killing seven iron golems? (6,4)

**2** If a villager is selling two lapis lazuli for one emerald, how many lapis lazuli could I get with four emeralds? (5)

**3** If a zombie drops zero to two pieces of rotten flesh when it dies, what's the maximum rotten flesh you can get from killing two zombies? (4)

**4** If a villager is selling six apples for one emerald, how many apples can you buy for three emeralds? (8)

**5** If you need four string to craft one white wool, how many string do you need to craft three white wool? (6)

# 50 Crossword

### Across
1 Achievement you obtain by curing a zombie villager (6,6)
5 Minecraft creature (3)
7 Drop from a ghast which is a crafting ingredient for an end crystal (5,4)
9 Decorative transparent block (5)
10 Type of villager who makes arrows (8)
11 Drop from a squid which can be used to make dye (3,3)
12 Villager who makes tools, armor or weapons (10)

### Down
2 Achievement you gain by creating an iron golem (4,5)
3 Baby polar bear (3)
4 Small hostile mob which can enter a nearby stone block, transforming it into a monster spawner (10)
5 Item which can be played in a jukebox (5,4)
6 "Weapon" which an Evoker can cause to rise up out of the ground (4)
8 What a villager turns into when lightning strikes within 3-4 blocks (5)

# Solutions

## 1 Crossword

## 2 Quizword

## 3 Crossword

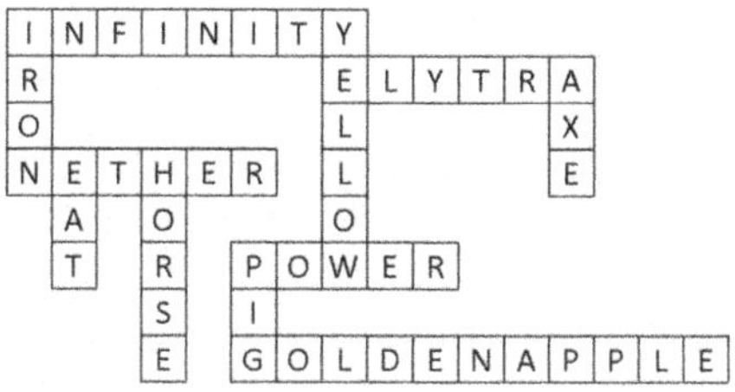

## 4 Crossword

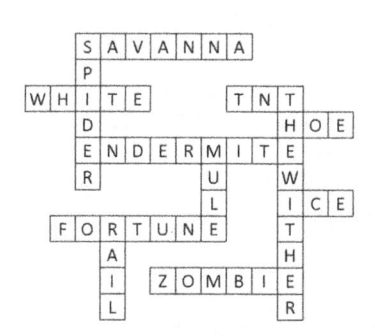

## 5 Crossword

## 6 Quizword

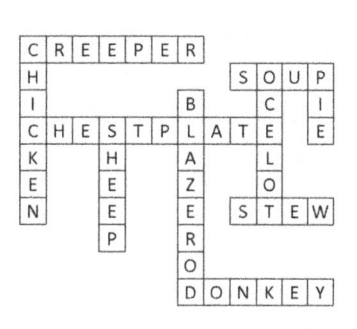

## 7 Crossword

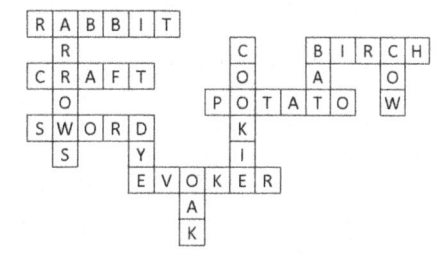

## 8 Crossword

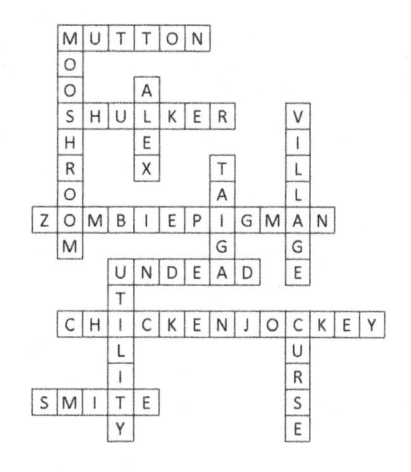

## 9 Quizword

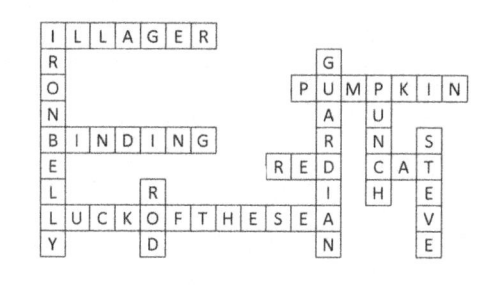

## 10 Crossword

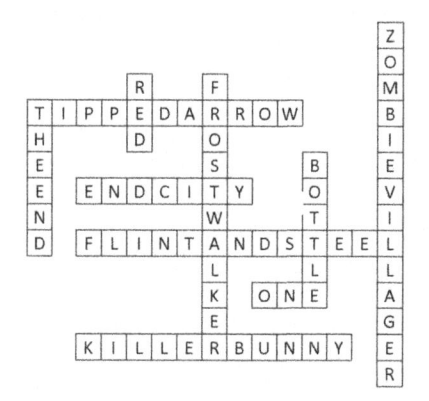

## 11 Quizword

## 12 Crossword

# Solutions

## 13 Crossword

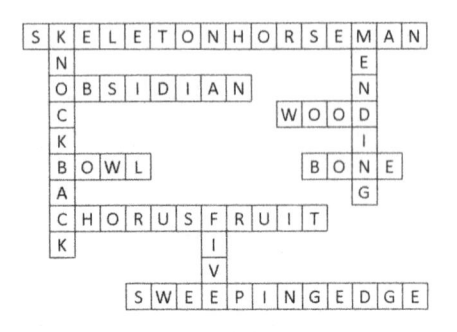

Across/Down grid:
- SKELETONHORSEMAN
- OBSIDIAN
- WOOD
- BOWL
- BONE
- CHORUSFRUIT
- SWEEPINGEDGE

Down words include: NOCKIAK, ENNIG, PLAIV

## 17 Numberword

- TWENTYEIGHT
- SIXTEEN
- FIVE
- TWO
- TEN
- SEVEN
- ONE

Down: SIXTH, THIRTY TWO, FOUR, EIGHTEEN

## 21 Crossword

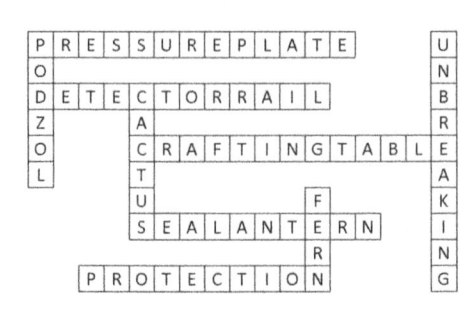

- PRESSUREPLATE
- DETECTORRAIL
- CRAFTINGTABLE
- SEALANTERN
- PROTECTION

Down: POOZOL, UNBREAKING, FIRE

## 14 Quizword

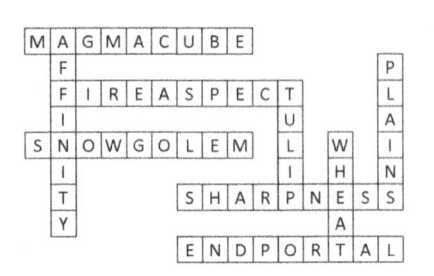

- MAGMACUBE
- FIREASPECT
- SNOWGOLEM
- SHARPNESS
- ENDPORTAL

Down: FITY, FUULI, WHIA, PLAIN

## 18 Crossword

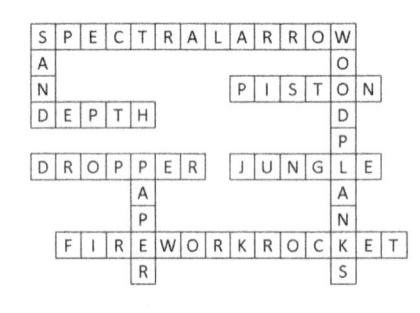

- SPECTRALARROW
- PISTON
- DEPTH
- DROPPER
- JUNGLE
- FIREWORKROCKET

Down: SAND, WOOD, DPAPR, OANS

## 22 Numberword

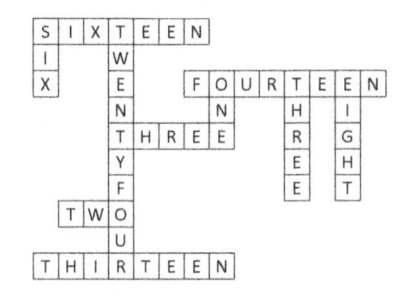

- SIXTEEN
- FOURTEEN
- THREE
- TWO
- THIRTEEN

Down: SIX, WENTY, EN, ENYFOU, NHRGHT, IEE

## 15 Crossword

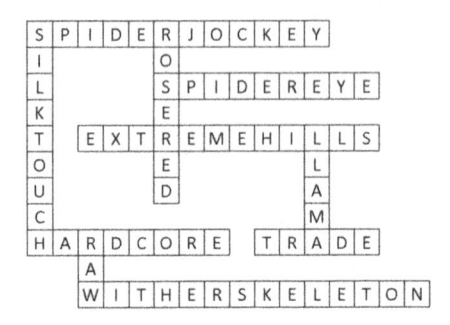

- SPIDERJOCKEY
- SPIDEREYE
- EXTREMEHILLS
- HARDCORE
- TRADE
- WITHERSKELETON

Down: SILK TOUCH, OOSEED, LAM

## 19 Crossword

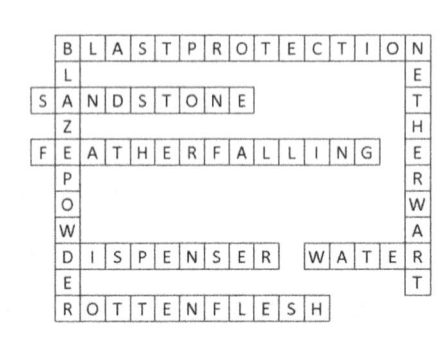

- BLASTPROTECTION
- SANDSTONE
- FEATHERFALLING
- DISPENSER
- WATER
- ROTTENFLESH

Down: BLIZZPOWDER, NETHERWART

## 23 Crossword

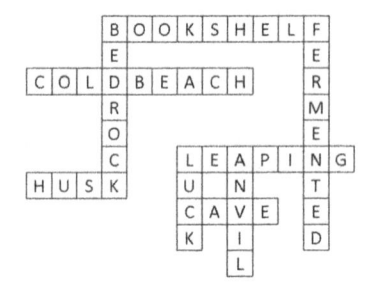

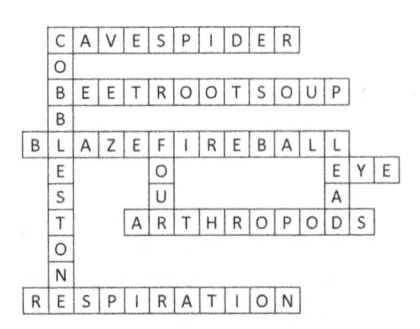

- BOOKSHELF
- COLDBEACH
- LEAPING
- HUSK
- CAVE

Down: BEEROCK, FERMEETED, UNTIL

## 16 Crossword

- CAVESPIDER
- BEETROOTSOUP
- BLAZEFIREBALL
- EYE
- ARTHROPODS
- RESPIRATION

Down: COBBLESTONE, OU A

## 20 Crossword

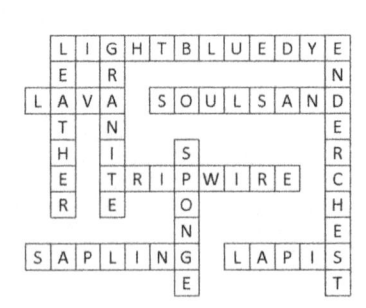

- LIGHTBLUEDYE
- LAVA
- SOULSAND
- TRIPWIRE
- SAPLING
- LAPIS

Down: LEATHER, ENDERCHEST, STONE

## 24 Quizword

- PURPURBLOCK
- SWIFTNESS
- REDSTONE
- NETHERPORTAL
- MOSSSTONE

Down: PRISMARIN, ON, COAX

# Solutions

## 25 Crossword
- DAYLIGHTSENSOR
- DONKEY
- ADDER
- STRENGTH
- SWAMPLAND
- MELEE
- MINE
- PARROT
- SPLASH

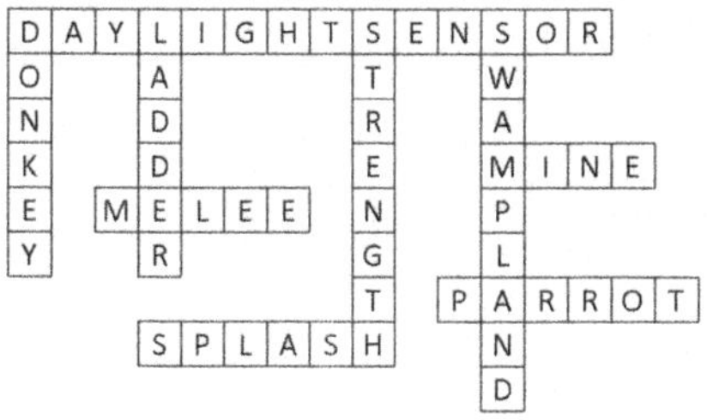

## 26 Crossword
- MONSTEREGG
- MYCELIUM
- REDSTONETORCH
- TRAPDOOR
- EXPLODE
- HOPPER
- CREATIVE
- TWO
- TEN
- VEX

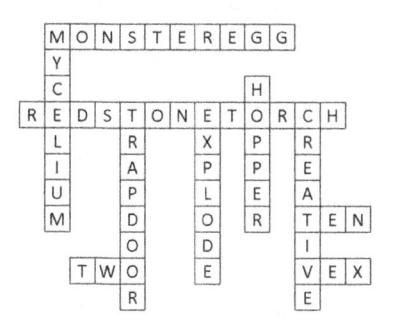

## 27 Crossword
- FIRERESISTANCE
- CEEPLAINS
- REGENERATION
- WEAKNESS
- SLIME
- DANDELION
- COBWEB
- BLOCK
- VISION
- NETHERRACK

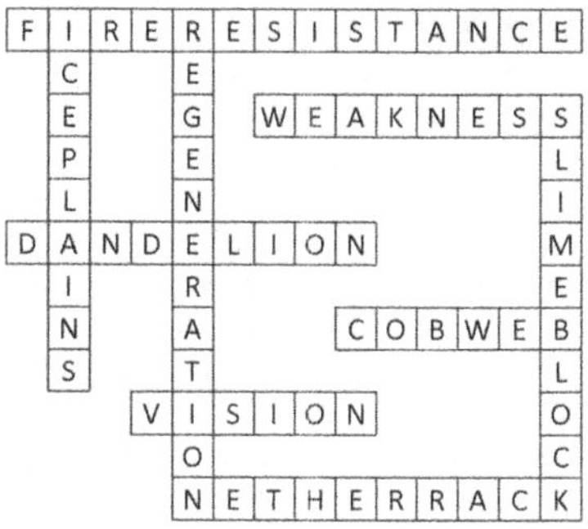

## 28 Numberword
- EIGHTYSEVEN
- EIGHT
- THREE
- TWENTYSEVEN
- SEVEN
- ONE
- ELEVEN
- NINE
- TEN

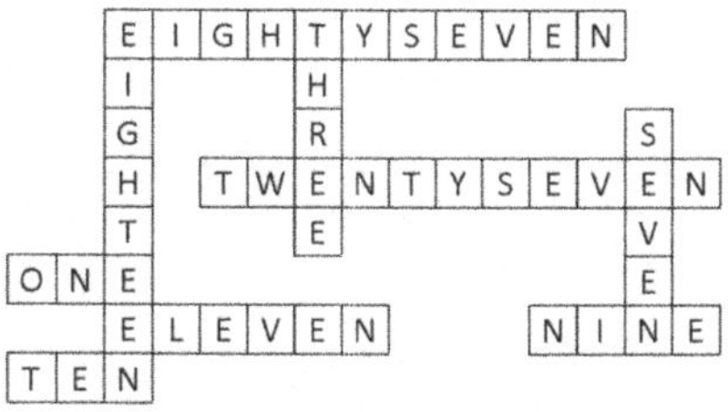

## 29 Quizword
- JORDANMARON
- PAUL
- JACK
- LOVEMODE
- DRAGON
- PURPLE
- WATERBREATHING
- WITHER
- BONEMEAL
- ENDERDRAGON

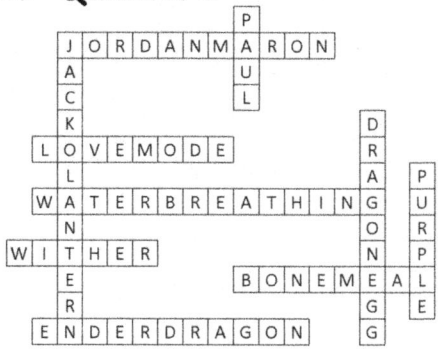

## 30 Crossword
- DANTDM
- JET
- STONE
- BLOCK
- DURABILITY
- ARMORSTAND
- ICEPLAINSSPIKES
- INVISIBILITY

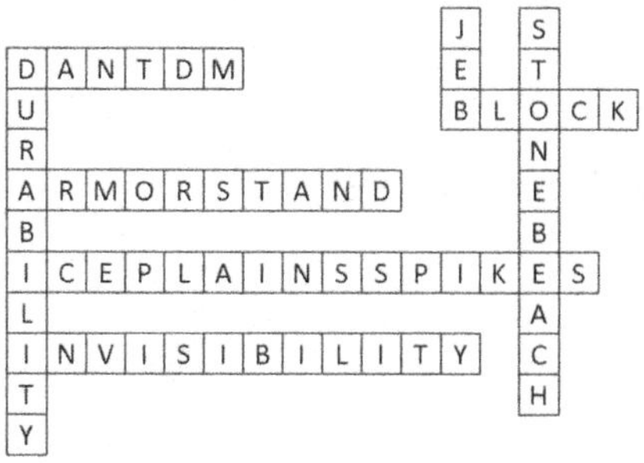

## 31 Crossword
- PRISMARINECRYSTAL
- POISON
- OW
- SLOWNESS
- HITCHHUG
- BEACON
- NETHERBRICK
- DIORITE
- NOTCH

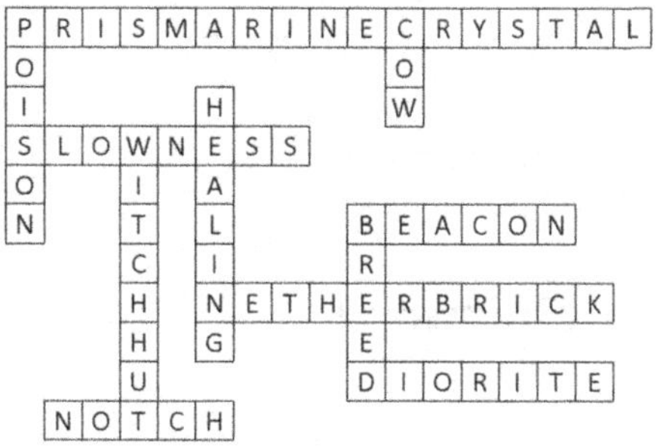

## 32 Crossword
- SHOVEL
- ACTIVATOR
- DIRT
- SHINESS
- GLOWSTONE
- HEIGHT
- RANG
- CLAY
- GRAVEL

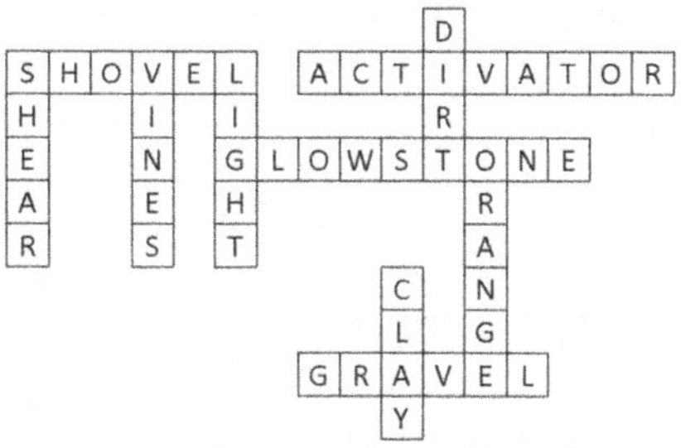

## 33 Numberword
- FIFTEEN
- FIVE
- FOUR
- EIGHT
- NINE
- THREE
- TWENTY
- TEN
- TWO

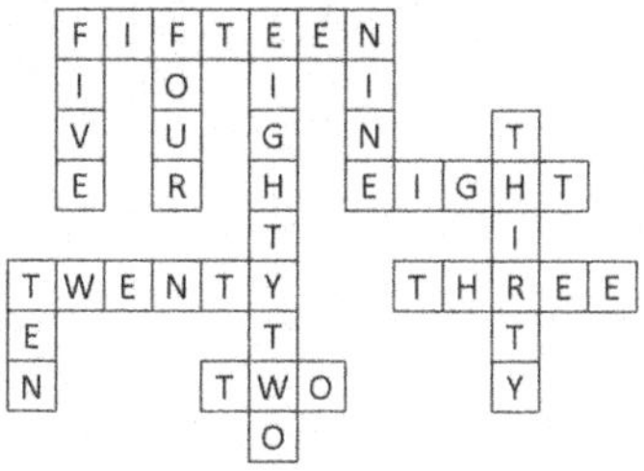

## 34 Crossword
- POISONOUSPOTATO
- PUMPKINSEEDS
- MINECART
- CHEST
- WHEATSEEDS
- ZOMBIE
- ENCHANTMENT
- SADDLE

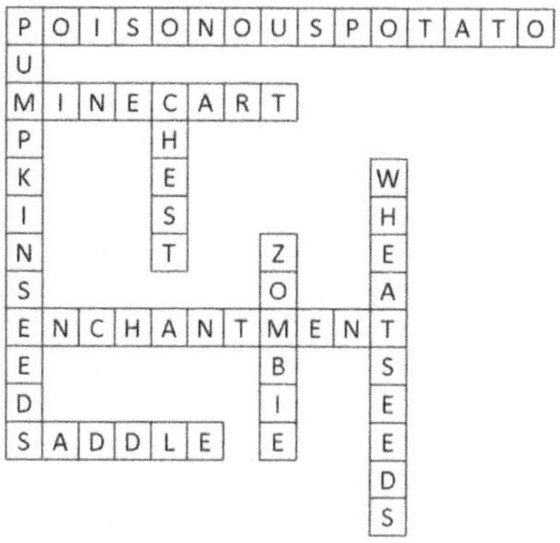

## 35 Quizword
- CHARGEDCREEPER
- CAULDRON
- UNO
- ICE
- SPIT
- PINK
- AXE
- WOLF
- SEEDS
- FARMLAND
- RUN

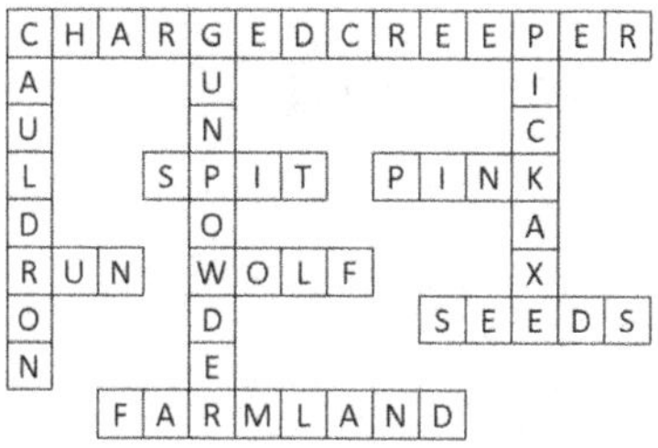

## 36 Crossword
- DESERT
- BREWINGSTAND
- BIOME
- EMERALDORE
- TNT
- TAIGA
- COUCH
- SPIDER
- EGG

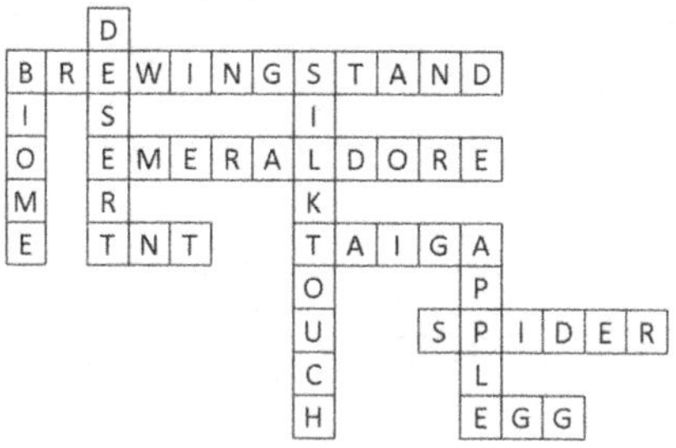

## 37 Crossword
- PASS
- ENDERMAN
- BEETROOT
- PASSIVE
- BLAZE
- CARROT
- FORTUNE
- TAMEABLE
- ROTTEN
- MELONSEEDS

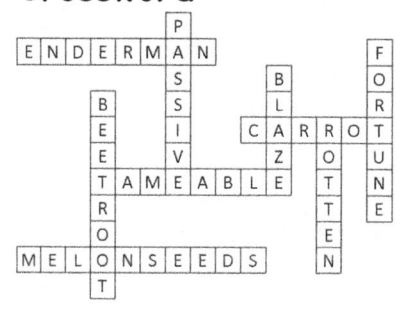

## 38 Crossword
- SHEEP
- COURSE
- SUNFLOWERPLAINS
- SUPERFLAT
- OBSIDIAN
- SAND
- FOOD
- DIRT
- JUNGLE
- THREE

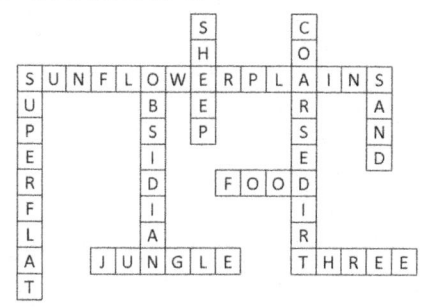

# Solutions

## 39 Crossword

## 43 Crossword

## 47 Quizword

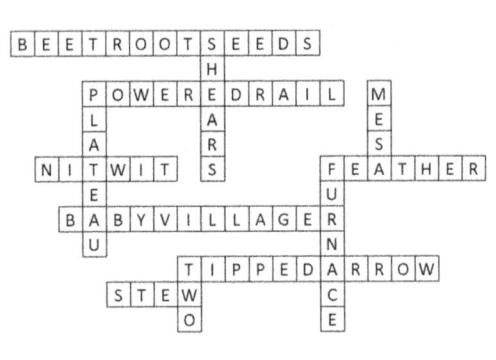

## 40 Crossword

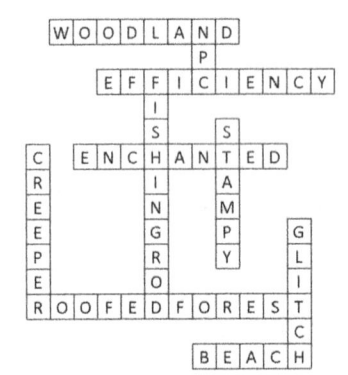

## 44 Crossword

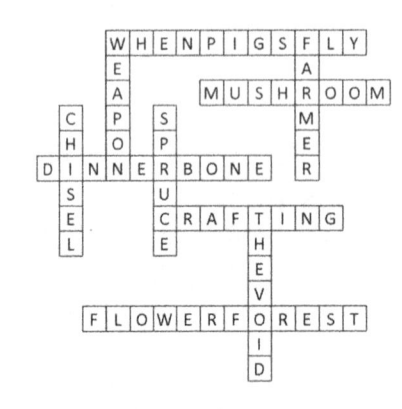

## 48 Crossword

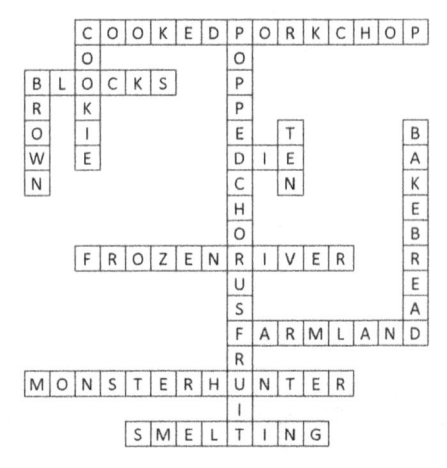

## 41 Crossword

## 45 Quizword

## 49 Numberword

## 42 Crossword

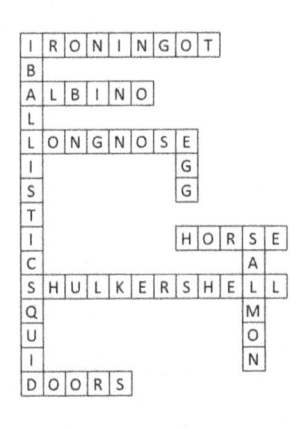

## 46 Crossword

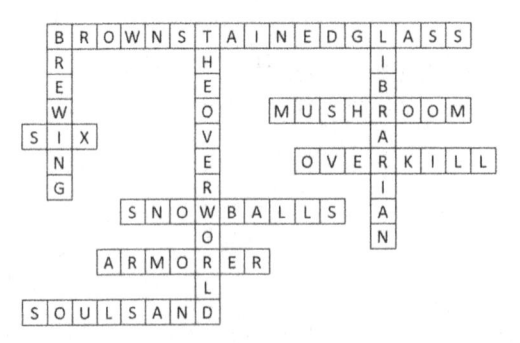

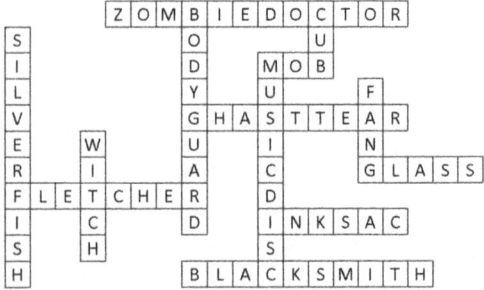

## 50 Crossword

Made in the USA
Monee, IL
12 December 2019